Walk Your Talk

Walk Your Talk

Grow Your Business Faster Through Successful Cross-Promotional Partnerships

Kare Anderson

SPIRAL PUBLISHING

Distributed to the trade by
CELESTIALARTS
Berkeley, California

Manufactured in the United States of America

Cover and text designed by David Charlsen
Text composition by ImageComp

If you would like information about having Kare Anderson speak at a conference, community or in-house meeting she can be reached at:
1-800-488-5273 (KARE)
or you can write to:
Spiral Publishing
15 Sausalito Blvd.
Sausalito, CA 94965

Distributed to the trade by: Celestial Arts
                                      P.O. Box 7123
                                      Berkeley, CA 94707

Library of Congress Catalog Number: 93-087451

ISBN: 0-89087-742-4

If you wish to obtain additional copies of this book, please check your local bookstore or refer to the Order Form on page 216.

2 3 4 5 6 7 8 — 99 98 97 96 95 94

TABLE OF CONTENTS

PART ONE

A NEW APPROACH TO
CHOOSING AND WORKING WITH PARTNERS

PART TWO

PRACTICAL WALK YOUR TALK CROSS-PROMOTIONAL IDEAS

Walk Your Talk

PART ONE

A NEW APPROACH TO CHOOSING AND WORKING WITH PARTNERS

MARKETING MAGIC: A NEW APPROACH

Last Valentine's day, six neighborhood businesses joined forces for a week-long promotion. The bookstore hosted cooking demonstrations by the author of a book on romantic meals, who used cookware from the local department store and food from the nearby deli. The finished meals were displayed with offerings from the local florist, candy store, and card shop — and health information from the Heart Association!

This is not an isolated incident. This is a growing phenomena. It is the next wave of marketing "technology." Businesses are discovering that in an increasingly tough, competitive environment they need to join allies in reducing their costs, expanding their markets, building community good will and keeping their customers forever. You can be a part of this new alliance by utilizing Walk Your Talk cross-promotions.

WALK YOUR TALK MAGIC AT WORK

- The newest location for fast food outlets is . . . inside convenience stores. Some 7-11s now have a Hardee's, and Dunkin' Donuts are served in several Circle Ks. Burger King sells hamburgers in selected Woolworth stores.

- A box of decongestant tablets carries a discount coupon for tissues, so shoppers looking for "nasal relief" may be prompted to buy both items.

- A lawyer and CPA teamed up for a humorous, informative talk to civic groups on "Know Your Money, Know Your Rights" that grew into a newspaper column and local talk shop segment — and also brought them both a 15-20% increase in clients.

- Young mothers in Pittsburgh learned how to get their kids immunized when they visited a diaper service or neighborhood children's clothing shop — and even earned discounts if they showed proof that their youngsters had received the shots.

- A video store owner gave free rentals to a nursing home and showed educational tapes in grammar schools, earning the good will and business of the seniors' adult children and the school kids' parents.

- A dry cleaner offered "frequent-dryer" credits that customers could apply either to their own future cleaning or to cleaning the local high school's band and sports uniforms.

- The mayor galvanized his whole community behind a Big Brothers and Sisters program, bringing together businesses, nonprofits, and government agencies in a joint promotion that had people clamoring to participate, and gave every group involved a promotional shot in the arm.

What these people all have in common is the art of Walk Your Talk cross-promoting. They reached more people, more often, more effectively, for less money — and in some cases they also got to contribute to their communities.

Walk Your Talk cross-promoting with allies who want to reach the same people you do is an imaginative, cost-efficient, highly effective way to get the word out about your product or service — whether you are Jerry's Video Rental, the local McDonald's or GAP manager, the new dentist in town, the area Cancer Association, the PTA, or the city health service.

WHAT IS WALK YOUR TALK CROSS-PROMOTING?

Walk Your Talk cross-promoting means pooling your promotional resources (time, money, ideas, contacts, etc.) with others who share the same market, so that everyone gets more visibility and positive impact for a fraction of the effort and expense. The result is that your present customers and clients keep coming back, and new people are drawn to you.

Walk Your Talk cross-promotion might involve a joint advertising campaign, media event, or mailing; offering discounts on one another's products or services; promoting one another with signs or flyers in your places of business; or having the Blue Angels write your names across the sky.

It can be anything that you and your partner think will capture the attention of the customers you share — and it's limited only by your imagination.

A NEW WAY OF THINKING . . .
FROM THE INSIDE OUT

This book offers a new approach that makes Walk Your Talk cross-promoting even more powerful and personally rewarding. It is based on a new way of thinking . . . from the inside out.

> After the excesses of the 1980s, we are moving away from greed, naked self-interest, manipulation, and wild spending. We want more connection and cooperation, more collaboration and mutual support. We are gravitating toward genuine core values, efficient and thoughtful use of our resources, authentic and honest relationships. We want to create community, to make our towns and cities better places to live. We want to help one another, and also succeed at what we do.
>
> Walk Your Talk cross-promoting in this new way lets you do just that. In *The Seven Habits of Highly Effective People* (Fireside, 1990) and *Principle-Centered Leadership* (Fireside, 1992), Steven Covey advocates beginning with your personal core values, and then making your outward actions an extension of those inner principles. This new approach to Walk Your Talk cross-promoting also works from the inside out.

You start with the core of your business or organization — your customers — and learn as much as you can about them. How specific can you get about who they are, what they want and value, where they go, what they read, and where they spend their time and money when they are not with you? Then you ask who else wants to reach that same audience. Which businesses, nonprofit organizations, or government agencies serve the same people you do? These are your natural Walk Your Talk cross-promoting partners.

You also look at your organization from the inside out. What do you stand for? How well does your product or service fulfill your customers' needs and wants? What can you do to serve them better? What do you want your organization to represent in the world?

When you know exactly who your market is and who you are, you can plan your outreach in a more thoughtful, targeted way. You can literally go where your customers go when they are not with you, and approach the other people who have contact with them. You can work with those people to reach your mutual audience, carrying a message that means something both to you and to your customers, so that everybody wins — you, your partner, and the people you both serve.

Basically, you ask three questions:

1. Who are my customers?

2. Who else wants to reach those same people?

3. How can we reach and serve them most effectively?

The power of this new approach is MUTUALITY, and it reflects the new spirit of cooperation and genuine contribution that is taking root across America. You choose partners with whom you share **mutual markets**, and energize your alliance with **mutual benefits**. You plan promotions that reflect your **mutual concerns**, and enjoy **mutual success**.

The more clear you are about your relationships with others — customers, colleagues, vendors, and other organizations — the more your business succeeds. You do good, you feel good, and you get the results you want. That turns a proven concept, Walk Your Talk cross-promoting, into marketing magic.

MUTUAL MARKETS: WHERE THE MAGIC BEGINS

Bob and Ted, the lawyer and CPA mentioned at the beginning of this chapter, were college friends who had both been in practice for about ten years and wanted to increase their client bases. They had dinner one night after racquetball to discuss how they could help one another. As they talked about who their current clients were and what kinds of people they wanted to attract, Bob and Ted realized that their markets were almost identical. Nearly all of Bob's clients were potential clients for Ted, and vice versa — and their prospective clients looked remarkably similar as well.

The advantages of actively referring clients back and forth to one another were obvious, but Bob and Ted also saw that they could work together to attract new clients — and have some fun in the process. What they had always enjoyed most about one another was their humor, so they put together an amusing talk for civic groups about when to use an attorney and when to use a CPA — "Know your Money, Know your Rights."

The presentation was so successful that they started writing a newspaper column by the same title. A television producer saw them at Rotary and gave them a weekly segment on a local talk show. Bob and Ted became minor celebrities, and took their work to new levels of success and fun.

MUTUAL MARKETS like Bob and Ted's are the cornerstone of every successful Walk Your Talk cross-promotion. This new approach means shifting from **product-based** thinking to **people-based** thinking. You concentrate on **who your customers are** rather than on **what you are providing them**.

Whether you are offering bagels, driver's licenses, screwdrivers, or health information, the first step is to get specific about who uses your product or service, when, how, where, and why. The more you know about your customers and clients, the better partners you will choose — and the more effective your Walk Your Talk cross-promotions will be.

Your partner's organization may be very different from yours. Good Walk Your Talk cross-promoting partners don't have to look, sound, or act alike; they just have to share the same market.

Helen owned a diaper service. Each morning as she drove past Janet's Wee Folk Clothing Store, it occurred to her that they probably shared a market: mid- to upper-income parents of infants. When she finally worked up the courage to call Janet, they discovered that they even had some of the same names on their mailing lists.

Janet and Helen immediately saw that they could both benefit by combining forces, and targeted their mutual market by offering one free diaper service with the purchase of $100 worth of clothing. They split the cost of providing the free diaper service and placing the ad, and both businesses experienced a substantial rise in sales. The next year, they teamed up with the health department and made immunization information — and discounts with proof that children had gotten the shots — available in both shops.

The diaper service, trendy clothing store, and health department looked very different from one another on the surface, but made excellent Walk Your Talk cross-promoting partners because they shared the same market.

MUTUAL BENEFITS:
PARTNERSHIPS FOR FUN AND PROFIT

Alliances based on this new approach are profitable because you target your market so precisely, and fun because they are powered by MUTUAL BENEFITS and support.

When you and your partner share the same market, you have an instant, natural common ground. You both know exactly where your common interest lies, and can channel all your energy in that direction. You are essentially saying to one another: "We are both targeting this specific group of people. How can we best do that?"

Barbara put her flower shop on the map by keeping up with who her customers were and what they wanted — and by staying on the lookout for other businesses and organizations whose products or services were important to those people. On December 1, she sent an intriguing note to the managers of the neighboring bookstore, card shop, deli, candy store, and department store, as well as to the director of the local Heart Association: "We have something in common. Come to my place for lunch at noon on December 8 and find out what it is."

She opened the lunch by asking if anybody knew what they all had in common, and this savvy group quickly recognized that almost everybody around the table sold Valentine's Day products. They smiled when they realized that the other luncheon guests also had an interest in hearts, and recognized immediately that they could all benefit by working together. They wanted everyone in town to "Think Hearts," and that became the slogan for their week-long Walk Your Talk cross-promotion. The visual signature that they used on posters and flyers in one another's stores was a big, bright-red heart.

The bookstore owner volunteered to contact the "romantic meal" author and to host cooking demonstrations that also featured the other partners' offerings: flowers, cards, cookware, deli food, and health information. They got more media attention because the Heart Association was included, and their Valentine's Day promotion became a tradition that also led to friendships and supportive professional alliances which continued throughout the year.

By working with partners in a spirit of genuine support and cooperation based on mutual benefit, you are constantly strengthening alliances and building new ones. Again, you're working "from the inside out." You nurture a sense of community and create positive energy.

Your organization succeeds, your partners' organizations succeed, your clients and customers are served better, and your community is stronger because people have come together to help and promote one another.

MUTUAL CONCERNS: WHAT DO YOU STAND FOR?

MUTUAL CONCERNS are another way that this new kind of Walk Your Talk cross-promotion works "from the inside out." You know what you stand for, so you can plan promotions that reflect your own values, the genuine needs of the people you serve, and the principles that your organizations represent.

We make statements with our organizations, and those statements should match our personal core beliefs. You and your partner don't have to share exactly the same beliefs and goals, but you should know what one another stand for and your motivations shouldn't conflict. You should be able to support one another's principles and aims, even if you each have your own agenda.

Tom's first impulse after reading about Walk Your Talk cross-promotion was to race out, grab three partners from among the merchants in his block, and blanket the neighborhood with flyers that advertised their businesses. He stopped himself because the gesture felt empty and somewhat crass. Instead, he spent the afternoon writing detailed profiles of his video store's customers and potential customers so that he could choose partners who shared those markets. He also asked himself the following questions:

- What do I really want from this business?

- How important is it to have fun and do good, as well as to produce results and make money?

- What statement do I want my video store to make?

Tom's "inside job" revealed that he wanted to tap his hidden markets of elderly people and school children, and also that it was important for his business to contribute in some way to these groups. He talked first with Eleanor, who was the director of a nursing home. They saw that it would benefit both of them for Tom to loan tapes to residents without charge. The nursing home got a wonderful new entertainment resource at no cost, and Tom got the personal satisfaction of making a contribution; the good will of residents' families, friends, and visitors; and the support of senior citizens outside the home who heard about what he was doing from their friends or from an article that appeared in the paper.

The Walk Your Talk cross-promotion was so successful that Tom did a similar one with the local grammar school, showing tapes that taught children how to cope with strangers on the street. The principal was delighted because the school could provide an additional service, and Tom scored points with the kids' parents and also got exposure with a young potential market.

Working "from the inside out" made Tom feel good about himself and also made his business more successful. Examining how he wanted to relate to his community led to a contribution, and that contribution led to more business.

Walk Your Talk cross-promoting based on your personal core values doesn't mean you have to save the world, although being socially responsible is now one of the best ways to get people's positive attention. It just means planning promotions that interest and excite you, rather than merely going through the motions.

Madeline owned a dry cleaning business and was an avid fan of the local high school's football and baseball teams. She also realized that she and the school shared the "market" of the kids' parents, and sat down with Calvin, the athletic director, to talk about a plan that could benefit both of them. They came up with a "frequent-dryer" program in which her customers would earn credits that they could apply either to their own future cleaning or to an account for cleaning the school's band and sports uniforms.

The athletic department saved money and Madeline was acknowledged prominently in programs distributed at the games. This Walk Your Talk cross-promotion didn't change the course of human history, but both Madeline and the high school benefited. Madeline's contribution came from the heart, her business flourished, and she got a big kick out of being associated with the teams.

MUTUAL SUCCESS: FOUR WAYS TO WIN

Another unique feature of this new approach to Walk Your Talk cross-promoting is that it includes four groups that don't always cooperate with one another, and shows them how to work together **at the local level**:

1. Small businesses

2. Local outlets of national concerns

3. Nonprofit organizations

4. Government agencies

Small businesses often cross-promote only with other small businesses, government agencies with other agencies, nonprofits with other nonprofits. Local outlets of national concerns can get stuck in the trap of only using promotions handed down from headquarters, and miss chances to speak directly to local people and carve out a niche for themselves in the community.

This new approach advocates crossing those invisible lines and forming new alliances with other kinds of organizations for MUTUAL SUCCESS. You extend yourself more deeply into the community, so you gain access to people you might not otherwise reach.

By concentrating all your energy at the local level, you combine the proven technique of co-op marketing with the new concept of "narrowcasting" or targeting a narrow local market with messages that are specific to their situation:

- "All you commuters struggling up Route 101 on your way to work in San Francisco this morning, take BART (Bay Area Rapid Transit) tomorrow, read your *San Jose Mercury News* in peace and comfort, and arrive at the office cool, calm and collected."

- "We know how hot it's been in Elmhurst this summer. That's why the DuPage County Health Department urges you to drink lots of water and take it easy — and why you get a free medium-sized soft drink at Tastee-Freeze each time you leave K-Mart with more than $20 worth of merchandise."

These innovative community-based Walk Your Talk cross-promotions among small businesses, local outlets, nonprofits, and government agencies can be:

SIMPLE COLLABORATIONS BETWEEN TWO PARTNERS ... The local Cancer Association teams up with a restaurant offering healthy meals to teach people about low-fat, high-fiber diets.

MORE COMPLEX, COMMUNITY-WIDE EFFORTS INVOLVING MANY PARTNERS . . . The mayor of a mid-sized town used creative Walk Your Talk cross-promotion instead of a big budget to get the word out about his Big Brothers and Sisters program. He thought of other people who reached the same group he wanted to reach — socially responsible, relatively affluent, predominantly young and single adults with some spare time — and wasn't afraid to cross the lines among business, nonprofits, and government. He set up a meeting with the managers of a copy shop, a bank, three restaurants, a health club, two department stores and other retail outlets; a hospital community relations director; public relations directors of two large national corporations that had offices in town; the public service director of the community's top radio station; and the head of the city's public transportation system.

Everyone agreed that cooperating to promote the Big Brothers and Sisters program would not only help the community, but enhance their own images with an audience that was important to them. By pooling their resources, they could reach their targeted market quickly and effectively at very little cost.

The copy shop printed colorful flyers telling potential Big Brothers and Sisters how to get involved, and its contribution was acknowledged at the bottom "as a public service." The flyers were placed in Plexiglas stands in the bank, restaurants, health club, busses and rapid transit trains, department stores, and hospital and corporate cafeteria cashier stands. Each organization participating in this outreach was acknowledged on the flyer as a sponsor, and the radio station mentioned them in its public service announcements about the program.

Everyone in town heard these spots and saw the flyers, and all the sponsors got positive exposure for supporting a worthwhile cause. The response from Big Brother and Sister volunteers was overwhelming, the mayor looked like a prince, each organization involved polished its public image, and all concerned had a sense of contributing to their community.

Other organizations clamored to join the Walk Your Talk cross-promotion, and a few months later the group took on two more partners. The local outlet of a national fast food company offered a free lunch to kids who came in with their Big Brothers or Sisters, and a bowling alley gave them 50% off on their first three lanes.

A NEW WAY TO CROSS-PROMOTE: THE FOUR Ps

This new approach to Walk Your Talk cross-promoting is a simple matter of four Ps. Here's how it works:

PEOPLE (MUTUAL MARKETS): You always begin by identifying your markets, the people who use or might use your product or service. Who are the people you serve? Whom do you want to reach? Find out as much as you can about age, sex, income, marital status, address, etc. What do they value most? What interests them? How do they think, feel, and act? Where do they get their information? How do they spend their time and money when they aren't doing business with you? Choose Walk Your Talk cross-promoting partners who want to reach those same people, so your partnership grows out of mutual markets.

PARTNERSHIPS (MUTUAL BENEFITS): Your partnership is based on reaching out to a specific group of people, so the mutual benefits are clear. As you talk, you'll probably find other common interests as well. Make sure you both know exactly what you stand to gain from supporting and cooperating with one another.

PURPOSE (MUTUAL CONCERNS): Your outreach reflects your personal values, mutual concerns, and the principles for which your organizations stand. Your promotions are driven not just by financial considerations, but by a genuine desire to relate in helpful, supportive ways to your customers, partners, and the community.

PROMOTIONS (MUTUAL SUCCESS): As you and your partners plan specific actions and promotions, you include all segments of the community — small businesses, local outlets of national concerns, nonprofit organizations, and government agencies — and stress their local connections to ensure mutual success.

Remember: Partners come together because they share **mutual markets**. Their collaboration begins by pinpointing their **mutual benefits**, and reflects their **mutual concerns**. Together, they develop promotions that bring **mutual success**.

HOW IT WORKS

Here is how the four Ps work in an actual Walk Your Talk cross-promotion:

Elizabeth was the advertising director at a radio station and Dave managed the local outlet of a national chain of home improvement stores. Both wanted to attract mid- and upper-income homeowners, who were a desirable demographic group for the station's advertisers and an obvious market for the store's products.

Dave and Elizabeth got together and created a ten-week "Energy Quiz" that featured questions about energy conservation in the home. Station DJs offered the quiz five times a day, along with tips on home improvement and saving energy. Dave created in-store displays that featured promos for the station and the quiz, and flyers listing "50 Tips for Home Energy Conservation." Winners received gift certificates at the store.

After the first successful quiz, Elizabeth and Dave drew in more partners from other segments of the community — an interior decorating firm, a kitchenware store, an alarm company, the local utility, the fire department, and the nonprofit Citizens for the Environment — for an expanded "Homeowner Quiz" with more questions, information, prizes, and in-store displays so that each partner got visibility in the other partners' places of business.

Each partner also got free advertising every time someone picked up the flyer or listened to the radio program, and they all earned a reputation for supporting the environment and working to conserve energy. Those who donated prizes were mentioned on the radio show every day and got far more positive exposure than they ever could have bought with the same amount of money. The radio program's ratings soared, and everyone in the community received a thorough, painless education in home energy conservation.

This Walk Your Talk cross-promotion enjoyed tremendous success because:

1. It was based on reaching mutual markets.

2. Each participant was clear on the mutual benefits.

3. The promotion itself grew out of mutual concerns.

4. It included small businesses, local outlets, nonprofits, and government agencies working together at the local level.

JUMPING IN

As you begin to think in terms of Walk Your Talk cross-promoting, you will see it everywhere:

- A huge supermarket chain, a hot dog brand, and a briquette company launch a joint advertising campaign around the Fourth of July.

- Cross sells pens to AT&T, which the telephone company gives away as gifts. The Cross ads say, "When AT&T recognizes excellence, everyone get the message. AT&T knows that gifts of Cross writing instruments are a memorable way to communicate its appreciation for a job well done." The words "message" and "communication" suggest that AT&T and Cross have something in common. AT&T cashes in on the Cross reputation for excellence; Cross rides the wave of AT&T's ubiquity and importance.

- Big John's Shoe Store has signs directing customers to Little John's Shoe Repair and Baby John's Shoe Shine.

You don't have to be a corporate giant with international connections and a billion-dollar advertising budget, or even be related to Big John, in order to cross-promote effectively. You just have to:

1. **Recognize that the principles of Walk Your Talk cross-promotion are there for anyone to use.** An interior designer and a hardware store can do the same kinds of things that Cross and AT&T do.

2. **Start thinking along Walk Your Talk cross-promotional lines.** Stay focused on your market, and be on the lookout for others who want to reach those same people.

3. **Remember that your ideas are special and unique.** You and your partner will create Walk Your Talk cross-promotions especially designed for your organizations, with your particular audience and community in mind. Trust yourself.

4. **Don't just think about it —** *do it.*

10 QUICK STARTERS

Start small and work into more complex Walk Your Talk cross-promotions as you gain experience. Here are ten quick, easy, inexpensive ways to start promoting with a partner:

1. Print joint promotional messages on your receipts.

2. Hang signs or posters promoting one another on your walls.

3. Put one another's business cards or promotional messages in Lucite stands on counters.

4. Drop one another's flyers in shopping bags.

5. Pool your mailing lists and send out a joint advertisement.

6. Share inexpensive ads in local shopping papers, school yearbooks, or theater programs.

7. Give a joint interview to local media, or mention one another when you are interviewed separately.

8. Encourage your sales staffs to mention one another ("If you need shoes to go with that dress, we recommend Hopkins on Seventh St.").

9. Print one another's names or messages on T-shirts, badges, arm bands, or hats worn by employees.

10. Use posters, flyers, or door hangers to promote discounts for one another's products or services.

USING THIS BOOK

Part I details this new approach to Walk Your Talk cross-promoting and helps you tailor it to your specific needs. Part II offers practical promotional ideas and shows how to make them work for your organization, in your community.

The information, exercises, and checklists in this book are designed to help you:

1. Pinpoint your best markets, discover new or hidden ones, and target those people more directly with clear, effective, personal messages.

2. Find your best allies and work effectively with them so that you enjoy energizing partnerships that enrich your own organization, contribute to others, and build community.

3. Know that you're doing right by yourself and others because you've thought about what you stand for and what you want.

4. Develop a joint market plan that keeps you focused and moving forward.

5. Create Walk Your Talk cross-promoting ideas and use the practical suggestions in this book.

SUMMARY

This fresh, innovative approach starts with the proven technique of Walk Your Talk cross-promotion, and turns it into marketing magic. It begins with defining your customers and choosing partners who share that audience. You then define the mutual benefits of working together and design creative Walk Your Talk cross-promotions that reflect your personal values and include all segments of the community.

CHAPTER 2

WHY
CROSS-PROMOTE?

Walk Your Talk cross-promoting not only lets you reach more people, more often, for less time, energy, and money — it also makes telling people about your product or service more fun. You're riding an upward spiral of energy, part of an inspired collaboration based on mutual markets and benefits, and aligned with authentic values and goals that prosper you, your organization, and your community.

While benefits and advantages to Walk Your Talk cross-promoting are multiple, varied and extend like ripples in a pond across your entire community, the bottom line is your business will grow faster and be more profitable.

WALK YOUR TALK BENEFITS

Personal: Since people come first in this new approach, you'll be looking for ways to strengthen relationships not only with your customers, but with your staff, your vendors, your colleagues, and your cross-promoting partners. You'll feel more connected to people, and may even want to include family or friends in some Walk Your Talk cross-promotions. You'll be bringing out the best parts of yourself as you work together, and being more supportive of everyone around you. Walk Your Talk cross-promoting is, in effect, a way to boast about one another — and that feels good to everyone.

Professional: You target your primary market more specifically than you have ever done, reaching more prospects, in more creative ways, more frequently, from more sides, with more credibility, for less money than is possible when you promote on your own. You build professional relationships, network with high-power allies, and become more influential in your community.

The Big Picture: You have a higher vision of what you want to do with your organization because you're working "from the inside out." You've looked at what's important to you, and that has probably resulted in contributing to your community, doing social good, and even becoming a role model for others. You feel better about yourself and have more fun.

In addition to these general benefits, there are some specific advantages to Walk Your Talk cross-promoting with this new approach.

WHAT YOU GET

Some of the advantages are obvious, and some are more subtle.

1. **You save money**. Sharing the expense makes everything you do more cost effective.

2. **You reach more people**. Walk Your Talk cross-promotion partners serve the same **kinds** of people you do, but they may not be

the same **people**. An up-scale clothing store and a gourmet deli may serve the same demographic groups, but have little or no duplication in their actual clientele. If they each have two hundred people on a mailing list and pool their lists, both reach twice as many people.

As you work with your partners to develop joint marketing plans, you will be constantly on the lookout for new ways to reach even more people and open up new markets.

3. **You reach people more often.** Usually, your exposure at least doubles — if only because your promotion is featured in both places of business.

4. **You and your partner can help one another through "slow times."** Most businesses and organizations have "up" and "down" times, periods of heavy activity followed by slow times of the day, week, month, or year. People may take clothes to the dry cleaner in the morning, for example, but only once or twice a month. They may buy ski clothes during the afternoon, but only in the late autumn. They may rent video cassettes more often on Friday than on other nights.

You and your partners can continue to promote one another through all of these peaks and valleys. In fact, you may want to look for partners whose rhythms of activity are different from yours.

5. **The focus shifts from your PRODUCT OR SERVICE to your CUSTOMER OR CLIENT.** Instead of asking "What do I have to sell?" you start asking, "Who wants to use or buy what I have?" Instead of telling customers why they should buy your product, you speak to them about **their** needs, values, interests, and concerns.

Finding Walk Your Talk cross-promotion partners is easy when you start thinking in terms of "Where else do my customers and clients spend their time and money? What else do they value? Where else do they go?" Shifting the focus **outward** to your customers and potential partners expands your vision and stimulates new ideas.

6. **You serve your customers and clients better.** Knowing more about your customers also lets you serve them better. Walk Your Talk cross-promotion encourages you to re-educate yourself not only about your customers and their needs, but also about your product and what your customers think of it. You learn why people do or do not use your product or service, and what you can do to improve it. You get into the habit of thinking, "How can I serve these people better?"

Good service ensures that your current customers remain happy and loyal — and they can be your strongest promoters.

7. **You move to the cutting edge of marketing in the 1990s.** In the 1980s, advertisers blitzed consumers with sales pitches, collectively spending more than $6 a week on every man, woman, and child in the United States, almost 50% more per capita than any other nation — and companies weren't entirely pleased with the return on their investment.

The 1990s brought a tough tactical and strategic reappraisal, with the goal of reaping more for less. Top marketing experts now pinpoint their audience and focus their message more clearly to produce a greater return on each marketing dollar.

Walk Your Talk cross-promotion at the local level encourages you to use these two key principles of contemporary marketing:

Target your audience very specifically. Knowing who your customers are is the foundation of Walk Your Talk cross-promoting. It's how you choose your partners and what drives your collaboration. You know exactly whom you want to reach, and can make excellent choices about where to target your promotion. Your efforts become more focused, efficient, and productive.

Speak to people in language that they understand. You know your customers' values, interests, and concerns, and can speak to them in meaningful ways. This is a chance to let your special hands-on knowledge and commitment work for you.

People respond best to creative, clever messages with a local angle that speak directly to them. When you cross-promote at the local level, you can rely on your own knowledge of your customers and your community to generate innovative marketing strategies.

8. **You buy outreach with imagination and creativity, not just money.** You don't need millions of dollars, advertising genius, or a fix on the hearts and minds of all America to make this approach work. You just need <u>common sense</u>, <u>creativity</u>, and <u>cooperation</u> — and some basic knowledge about your organization, your customers, and your community.

    When you get creative and trust your own unique ideas, there is no limit to what you can do.

9. **Your partnerships are based on solid, mutually supportive, and respectful collaboration.** Walk Your Talk cross-promotion is not about tricking, persuading or coercing others to promote your enterprise; it is about coming together as equals with people who want to reach the same people you do. Your mutual benefits and common goals are to increase your outreach, enhance your public image, and improve the quality of the products and services you provide. The partnership comes first; you develop the promotion together based on your mutual market and interests.

10. **You eliminate the "begging and buying off" pitfall of partnering with nonprofits.** Alliances between nonprofit organizations and businesses have often been a matter of nonprofits going begging and corporations doling out money, often in a condescending way, in order to buy off or co-opt criticism — from the nonprofit itself, from watchdog groups, or from the community at large. A utility or oil company might be less vulnerable to environmental charges, for instance, if it supports wildlife and wilderness organizations.

    When one partner gives and the other partner gets, the power is not equal — even when everyone has the best of intentions. This problem is minimized when partnerships are based on wanting to reach the same market. Each group contributes at least its own audience; no one arrives empty-handed, and everyone has something to gain.

    It's important for both parties to be clear about exactly what they are giving and receiving. Even when the nonprofit brings to the alliance more credibility, good will, time, energy, or public relations value than money, that positive exposure in the corporation's target market may be just as important to the corporation as the money is to the nonprofit — perhaps more so.

11. **You find unexpected allies and develop supportive relationships with other organizations.** Since **what** you are offering is less important than **to whom** you are offering it, you may find partners in unexpected places. The products or services that you and another organization offer may be very different, but if the people who use them are similar, then you may be perfect Walk Your Talk cross-promotional partners.

12. **It includes four diverse entities — small businesses, local outlets of larger national companies, nonprofit organizations, and government agencies —** working in a spirit of cooperation and generosity for authentic community outreach. Crossing the lines that separate business, nonprofits, and government can mean new contacts and relationships in all of these communities, more imaginative promotions, and vast new audiences.

13. **It is designed to be used at the local level** by organizations that serve a limited geographic area. This lets everyone target their specific audience more effectively, but can be particularly helpful to national organizations and large businesses with smaller outlets that need to establish links with the community and gain local support. Many national organizations are encouraging their outlets and franchises to cross-promote locally, for the simple reason that it is more effective and produces more revenue.

14. **You contribute to your community.** Whenever you join forces with another organization and reach out to others, you generate energy in your community. Contributing to your community feels good, and nothing makes you look better than giving something to the people of your city or town.

15. **Your promotions take on their own momentum.** When you work with partners over time, you don't have to keep reinventing the wheel. You can build on the energy and good will you've generated over the years, both between yourselves and with the

public. Your joint events and promotions may even become traditions in the community.

The work becomes easier, personal connections with Walk Your Talk cross-promotional partners become more fulfilling, and the promotions you do together reflect this spirit.

Walk Your Talk cross-promotion is more than good networking; it's a chance to develop personal trust and respect with other community leaders.

16. **You can join America's new promotional dream team: socially responsible businesses and uplifting worthy causes.** Enlightened self-interest brings out the best in everybody. When businesses that know how to promote for profit share their marketing savvy and outreach dollars with nonprofit organizations known for good works, everybody wins.

These businesses have an opportunity both to **do** good, and to be **known** for doing good when they cross-promote with inspiring health, social, environmental, or educational programs. The nonprofits get a promotional boost and a vast increase in the number of people who hear about their services.

This dynamic combination — **socially responsible businesses and uplifting worthy causes** — is fast becoming **the hottest Walk Your Talk cross-promotional duo of the decade** as both businesses and the public they serve realize that there is more to life than making money.

WHAT'S IN IT FOR YOU?

Everyone involved in Walk Your Talk cross-promotion reaps some or all of the above rewards, but each group also gets specific benefits.

. . . If You Are a Small Business

Small businesses include not only Harry's Auto Repair, Betty's Bakery, and local food stores, gas stations, book stores, dry cleaners, and video rental stores, but also:

- Lawyers, doctors, chiropractors, CPAs, and other professionals

- Local media, including television and radio stations, newspapers, billboards, and locally produced cable TV shows

The special benefits of Walk Your Talk cross-promotion to small businesses are that you increase sales by reaching more people, more often, for less money, while at the same time carving a unique niche for yourselves in the community.

You share the investments (time, money, and energy) and get a better return.

... If You Are a Large Business With a Local Focus

Local outlets, branches, and franchises of large businesses must foster a friendly, responsible, part-of-the-community image in the cities and neighborhoods they serve. These organizations include:

- The local outlets of such large retail concerns as McDonald's, GAP, Safeway, Bank of America, Chevron, and mail order businesses like the Banana Republic, Company Store, and L.L. Bean

- Telephone or utility companies

- Professional athletic teams

- Large corporations with a need for public support in the community where they are headquartered, especially if they are vulnerable to social or environmental criticism or to charges of being unfeeling corporate giants

Walk Your Talk cross-promotion with local small businesses, community nonprofits, and area government agencies can help these groups maintain a positive image with their various publics, which may include regulators, customers, community activists, and employees.

Alliances with local groups show the corporation's good intentions and give its employees a way to participate in the community —

perhaps by helping with an adult literacy program, taking a group of school kids to the country, working the phones at the local PBS station during pledge week, spearheading an environmental cleanup, or raising funds for a nonprofit day care center.

At the California-based Esprit clothing manufacturers, employees can use ten hours of company time a week to do volunteer work, as long as they match that with their own time. The company organized a volunteer fair to match up employees with civic groups, and makes grants of $100 to $10,000 for worthwhile community projects proposed by employees, who have come up with programs ranging from cuddling crack babies to planting trees.

The community benefits and employees feel good about both themselves and the company, which makes a genuine contribution and at the same time polishes its public image.

... If You Are a Nonprofit Organization

Nonprofits include:

- The local offices of such large organizations as the Heart Association, United Way, and Salvation Army

- Civic groups (Rotary, Chamber of Commerce)

- Local nonprofit associations such as child care centers, food banks, AIDS hospices, scholarships, and homeless funds

These organizations generally have less money to work with than businesses do, a high need to get the word out about the services they provide, and a desire to let potential contributors know how vital those services are.

Walk Your Talk cross-promotion frees nonprofits from the need to go begging for money, or to feel indebted when they do get funds. It gives them a way to become equal partners with businesses because they have something to give back — their audience and their good name. They also learn from their profit-oriented partners to see promotional opportunities they might have missed before, and to speak the language of business.

Forming alliances with other nonprofits and pooling resources to get the word out about both services is another way to benefit from Walk Your Talk cross-promotion.

. . . If You Are a Government Agency

This group includes:

- All city and county agencies and offices

- Schools (a potential partner with unlimited possibilities)

- Local offices of state or federal agencies (Agriculture Department, Department of Motor Vehicles, etc.)

Government cutbacks mean that fewer staff are being asked to provide more services with less money, so they need to use their time and resources more carefully and productively.

Three ways that government agencies can benefit from Walk Your Talk cross-promotion are:

- **Agencies** can do their jobs more efficiently and effectively by letting more people know about their services or requirements at less expense. For instance, the health department might work with businesses serving young people (clothing, video, and music stores) and with nonprofit drug programs to get information on AIDS into the hands of teens.

- **Employees** have a chance to make their jobs more interesting and creative through Walk Your Talk cross-promotion. They can get out and meet people in other sectors of the community, and develop new skills and contacts.

- **Officials** are more likely to be reappointed or re-elected if their administrations operate with more efficiency, productivity, and visibility.

Some ways that government agencies might cross-promote with businesses, nonprofits, and one another are:

- The Department of Motor Vehicles has information about nonprofit services for people to read while they wait in line. In return, the nonprofits make DMV forms available in their offices.

- The Small Business Administration distributes its information not only through small businesses, but through nonprofits and other government agencies that deal with new graduates or the unemployed.

SUMMARY

Walk Your Talk cross-promoting is a profoundly workable idea. Especially in lean and uncertain times, joining forces to promote your products or services:

- Enhances your visibility, your outreach, the quality and quantity of your service, and your good public image — without a huge promotional or advertising budget.

- Encourages relationships with other organizations and with your community that are practical, authentic, humane, and mutually beneficial.

CHAPTER 3

HOW TO CHOOSE GREAT WALK YOUR TALK CROSS-PROMOTING PARTNERS

Walk Your Talk cross-promoting partners will be small businesses, local outlets, nonprofits, and government agencies that want to reach the same people you do, so your first priority is to find out exactly who those people are.

I believe that only about 30% of small businesses and nonprofit organizations understand who their customers are. They may know something about why people use their product or service, but they rarely know what makes their customers tick or what those people do with the other 99% of their lives.

WHO ARE YOUR CUSTOMERS?

The key to choosing a good Walk Your Talk cross-promotion partner is understanding your clients' and customers' interests and values, and learning what they do, think, and feel when they aren't doing business with you.

Get as specific as you can about these important people. Who are they? How precisely can you describe the individuals who most need what you have to offer? Your best Walk Your Talk cross-promoting partners will be the people and organizations who serve, or want to serve, those same people.

The more clearly you can visualize your clients' lives, problems, passions, pursuits, and priorities — and then imagine who else might attract those same people for noncompetitive reasons — the better Walk Your Talk cross-promoting partners you will choose. Go where your customers go when they are not with you. Approach the other people with whom they interact — personally, professionally, financially, emotionally, socially, and in the areas of service — to be Walk Your Talk cross-promoting partners.

THREE HIDDEN BENEFITS OF REDEFINING YOUR AUDIENCE

Your customers or clients may be so familiar to you that you need to take a fresh look at them. Collecting accurate, updated, detailed information about the people you serve is not only the first step in selecting Walk Your Talk cross-promoting partners, it is good for business in three subtle ways:

1. **You know where to target your promotional message.** When you understand who your customers are, you know where they get their information and you don't throw money away by using media they never see or hear. If your audience consists exclusively of couch potatoes, for instance, you don't waste time and money advertising at sports events, gala evenings, or exercise facilities.

2. **You can align your messages with their most pressing needs, values, and interests.** The more you know about them, the more clearly you can speak their language and the more effectively you can capture their attention by talking about things that are important to them.

3. **You ensure the loyalty of current customers and clients.** You serve people better when you know more about them, and about what they want. The better you serve them, the more likely they are to keep coming back — and to bring their friends with them. It can cost five times as much to replace a customer as it does to keep one, and a dissatisfied customer tells more people about his or her experience than a satisfied one does. Keeping your current customers happy is one of the best investments you can make.

GET SPECIFIC

Here are two ways to describe the customers at a men's clothing store:

1. "Men who want dress shirts."

2. "Men between twenty and sixty-five who work in long-sleeved dress shirts and neckties. They know their size, buy between three and fifteen shirts a year (usually in the spring and autumn), and spend between $30 and $45 per shirt. The older men prefer all cotton, which they have professionally laundered. The younger men prefer cotton/polyester blends which they wash in laundromats and do not have to iron. During the Christmas season, a significant number of women buy shirts for the men in their lives. They are attracted to gift-wrapped displays."

Define your customers and clients in the most specific and concrete terms possible. Avoid abstractions. The more details you have, the more precisely you can target your market and the more effectively you can choose Walk Your Talk cross-promoting allies.

WHAT TO ASK: TWENTY QUESTIONS

What exactly do you need to know about your clients and customers in order to choose good Walk Your Talk cross-promoting partners? The following questions will help you develop a specific, accurate profile of the people you serve:

1. Are your customers men or women, or both?

2. How old are they?

3. What is their income?

4. Where do they live?

5. What are their occupations?

6. Do they have children?

7. What are their interests, values, and passions?

8. What do they have in common?

9. How do they spend their money?

10. How do they spend their time?

11. What do they talk or ask about most often?

12. How did they find you?

13. Why do they use your product or service?

14. Why have they chosen you over others who provide this product or service?

15. What is the one thing that they believe distinguishes your product or service from other similar ones?

16. How often do they use your service or buy your product?

17. When are they most likely to use your service or buy your product (times of day, days of week, seasons of the year)?

18. What other products and services do they use? Where do they find these products and services?

19. Where do they go before and after they see you?

20. What other businesses do they patronize when they are in your area?

WHOM SHOULD YOU ASK?

Where can you get the answers to these twenty questions?

1. Your customers and clients themselves are your best sources. They have the most complete and accurate information.

Many of them will be pleased and flattered that you show an interest, and will gladly answer your questions. Others may not want to take the time. Give them the option of answering questions verbally, completing a questionnaire at your place of business, taking the questionnaire home and mailing it back, or not answering the questions at all. Be sure to treat them in a friendly, respectful way regardless of their response.

Make it worth their while to answer your questions by offering a gift or discount to each person who fills out a questionnaire. One dentist gave free teeth-cleaning certificates, which patients could use themselves or pass on to a friend. Let your customers and clients know that you value their opinion, and that you respect their time and their views.

Drawings for prizes are another way to gather information about your customers. Put a large fish bowl near your cash register or reception area and announce that a special prize will be given away in thirty days. Have your customers fill out forms asking their name (to capture gender), birth date (to capture age) and address (to capture location). Enter this information in your database and update it frequently.

2. **Your employees** are also good sources of information about customers and clients. They speak directly to people who choose your business or organization, and may know some of them well. They can give you both hard facts and such subtle information as "People really hate the Beatles on our Muzak, but they like the show tunes."

3. **Use yourself as a resource, too.** Play detective. Go to work each day for a week as if it were the first time. Don't make any assumptions about the people you serve. Pretend that you are an independent researcher hired to pinpoint their demographics. Listen, watch, and ask questions.

FIND YOUR "MISSED MARKETS" — AND "MISSED PARTNERS"

Cast a wide net with your questions about who uses your product or service so that you don't miss any potential customers — or partners.

A toy store owner described his customers as "traditional families." A dry cleaner said his were "professional people." A hardware store manager called his customers "homeowners." These three businesses served essentially the same clientele and would have made excellent Walk Your Talk cross-promotion partners, but they all defined their audiences too narrowly — and none of them asked enough questions — to realize that.

These are some questions you might ask:

1. What kinds of people are similar to your current customers or clients, but may not yet be aware of your organization?

2. Where have you defined your customers and clients too narrowly? (The toy store owner who said his customers were "traditional families" also missed an opportunity to target divorced and other single parents.)

3. Can you list three groups of people who might be interested in your product or service that you have not yet targeted?

Cast a wide net for Walk Your Talk cross-promoting partners as well. Keep an open mind, and be alert for match-ups that are powerful, but unexpected.

If you and your partner are an unusual combination — two organizations that people wouldn't expect to see working together — then the partnership itself may attract attention, according to Robert Brandon, Chairman of the Promotion Marketing Association of America and head of his own Atlanta-based promotion company. "Walk Your Talk cross-promotions help companies get more bang for the buck out of their marketing budgets," says Brandon.

"Tax time relief" was the promise of a joint television ad that ran from February through mid-April 1987. As a man worked on his tax returns, he dropped two Alka-Seltzer tablets into a glass of water and telephoned H&R Block for help. A display ad in grocery and drug stores also linked Block and Alka-Seltzer as pain relievers.

Ask yourself these two questions:

1. If you could give your customers a coupon for discounts at another business or organization, what kinds of products or services would catch their eye or give them particular pleasure?

2. What kinds of businesses would benefit by giving their customers discount coupons for your product or service?

These may be your "missed partners."

WALK YOUR TALK CROSS-PROMOTION PARTNERS: A CHECKLIST

The goal of Walk Your Talk cross-promotion is to reach more people, more frequently, with creative messages that position your product or service in a favorable way with your target audience. You are looking for partners who will help you do that.

Choose Walk Your Talk cross-promotion partners on the basis of **whom they serve**, not **what they do**. You now know more about where your customers and clients go and what they do when they are not with you. **The people who provide these other products and services are your Walk Your Talk cross-promotion partners.**

As you read through the following checklist for choosing partners, write down the names of three potential partners who would satisfy that particular criterion.

Your best allies are:

1. Organizations that serve, or that want to serve, the same clients and customers you do — but that do not compete with you. These customers or clients may be:

> **People who share the same lifestyle** . . . They may enjoy the same activities, have the same interests or values, or be at the same stage of life.

> - Active, outdoor people might be the targets of Walk Your Talk cross-promotions by sports shops; fitness and exercise classes; health food stores; wilderness equipment and clothing outlets; tennis, golf, or swimming clubs; mail order training or equipment catalogs; trip, travel, and expedition clubs; and/or such environmental and conservation organizations as the Sierra Club and World Wildlife Fund.

> - New parents could be the audience for Walk Your Talk cross-promotions among baby food, clothing, equipment, and toys; life insurance; day care centers and preschools; and child education companies.

> - Recently divorced people might be courted by gyms and fitness salons; decorators; furniture and kitchen equipment stores; real estate agents; cooking classes; money management firms; and self-help classes and books.

> - People moving to a new city need almost everything: movers, painters, housecleaners, interior designers, furniture, yard

work and equipment, carpeting, take-out meals, maps, Chamber of Commerce information, and free introductory specials from any organization or business that wants to be remembered as an early friend in the new location. In one such promotion, real estate agents gave away "Welcome to Town" packets with tips from the school principal, coupons for landscaping and housecleaning, and invitations to the next civic event.

- Retirees are a good audience for investment companies; tour and travel agencies; and home medical equipment.

People who shop in the same way ... It is now possible for people with busy lives to choose between shopping in ways that save time (catalogs, television, computers, etc.) and spending a leisurely afternoon browsing through stores. Hooking up with people whose customers shop in the same way yours do can mean targeting your audience more directly and saving on advertising costs.

- When escalating postage and advertising costs threatened a French lace mail order company, the owner looked for other entrepreneurs who used direct mail and formed a cooperative. They saw the mutual benefit of trading mailing lists and customer profiles, and made plans to share the costs of printing and mailing.

Three potential Walk Your Talk cross-promotion partners that serve, or want to serve, the same people you do are:

1. _____

2. _____

3. _____

2. Organizations that serve people you want to attract. These groups may be just as interested in connecting with your customers and clients as you are in connecting with theirs, or you may be able to offer something else of value to them.

People who visit your potential partner's business, but have not yet connected with you ... Where do your customers go before and after they visit you? Where do they spend the rest of the day? Who else do they see that might be a good Walk Your Talk cross-promotional partner for you?

- The owner of a sports store was seated next to the owner of the local baseball team at a civic banquet. As Hal and Don talked, it dawned on them that they both served sports-minded people, but perhaps not the **same** sports-minded people. They realized that many people who currently went only to the store might also enjoy the games, and those who only went to the ballpark might also be interested in what the store offered. They saw the mutual benefit of connecting with new audiences and essentially trading customers. Hal and Don worked out a <u>no-cost</u> Walk Your Talk cross-promotion in which the team's announcer mentioned Don's shop several times during each game, and he sold tickets for the games at a discount in the store.

- Shelly was the Community Relations Director for St. Jude's Hospital and Pete ran the local blood bank. They met when Pete spoke at Shelly's professional association, and enjoyed talking to one another. They thought they would like working together, and realized that one group they both wanted to reach was potential blood donors. The benefit to the blood bank was obvious, and the hospital also benefited from an abundant blood supply and the good will generated by promoting blood donations.

  Since people visiting St. Jude's might be especially aware of the need for blood, the hospital advertised Pete's annual blood drive with signs and posters in the halls and lobbies. The drive was also mentioned in the hospital's monthly magazine, and Pete placed information on the hospital's services in his waiting room. <u>Blood donations increased 8%</u>, the hospital created good will and business, and an alliance was forged between St. Jude's and the blood bank that benefited both institutions for years to come.

People whom your potential partners reach easily, but whom you might have difficulty reaching . . . Sometimes Walk Your Talk cross-promotion is the only way to gain access to certain people. Look for partners who reach people in places where you are not.

- Luigi watched a hundred grammar school students walk past his pizza parlor on their way to the video arcade each day after school, and shook his head. How could he reach those kids? Two people had easy access to this primary market: the school principal and the arcade manager. Luigi introduced himself to the principal, Wes, and proposed a plan that targeted their mutual audience and benefited them both. Luigi would award free pizzas as prizes for academic achievement. Wes was delighted to provide this extra incentive at no cost, and Luigi smiled at the thought of this new, young market enjoying themselves in his establishment.

    After that Walk Your Talk cross-promotion was underway, Luigi proposed a similar plan to Arnold, the arcade manager. The kids with the highest scores on each machine at the end of each week would get a free pizza. Arnold realized that this competition would generate more business, and the kids once again found themselves at Luigi's.

Three potential Walk Your Talk cross-promotion partners who now serve people you want to attract are:

1. _____

2. _____

3. _____

3. Organizations whose good name lends prestige, credibility, or value to your promotion. These might include nonprofits that promote health, the environment, or other worthy causes; businesses with reputations for good performance and/or good works; government agencies whose names carry weight or credibility; or any group that has powerful, creative ideas for Walk Your Talk cross-promotions.

Before choosing a partner, make a list of what that organization will bring to your Walk Your Talk cross-promotion.

> The merchants' association at a mall wanted to do something to help hurricane victims, and knew that they needed to reach a fairly affluent, generous group of people who were likely to help with donations of food, clothing, and blankets — a market not unlike their own. They contacted the Red Cross, who knew how to access these people, and offered to collect the needed items at the mall and give discounts based on how much people contributed.
>
> Everybody benefited. The Red Cross got more donations. The merchants made a contribution, got credit for it, and experienced heavy traffic that weekend. People who brought supplies got discounts and also felt good about themselves. Everyone involved felt a greater sense of community, both locally and with the hurricane victims.

Three potential cross-promotion partners whose good name would lend prestige, credibility, or value to a Walk Your Talk cross-promotion are:

1. _____

2. _____

3. _____

4. Organizations that are geographically convenient to yours. Sheer proximity often suggests good allies. When customers are already in the area, it's easier for them to stop at your place of business. One of the best ways to encourage this is to be friends and partners with other businesses and organizations in your geographic area, and to take an active approach to recommending one another's product or service.

- "If you need shoes for this dress (or suit), you might try next door."

- "In addition to our workout classes, we always let people know about the diet program across the street."

Developers of shopping centers realized years ago that convenience is a strong selling point. They "anchored" malls with large department stores and filled in with specialty shops. A promotion for any one of these businesses drew potential customers to all of them.

Three potential Walk Your Talk cross-promotion partners geographically convenient to you are:

1. _____

2. _____

3. _____

5. Organizations whose "cycles" complement yours. Be sure you have updated, accurate information about your organization's cycles of high or low activity — certain times of the day, month, or year when people are most likely, or least likely, to use your products or services. Check this against your potential partners' cycles.

If your cycles are different, you can help one another out during slow times. A ski shop cross-promotes with Al's Bike Shop, advertising Al's spectacular sales in November, when few people buy bikes but everyone goes to the ski shop. Al returns the favor in the summer months.

Working with partners whose rhythms are different from yours can keep your product or service before people's eyes even when they aren't yet ready to use it. People who saw the advertising for Al's Bike Shop at the ski store all winter thought of Al first when the snow melted and they were ready to get back to cycling.

If your cycles are the same, you can join forces to make the most of your peak times. Christmas might bring together toy stores, the Salvation Army, nonprofits that sell Christmas trees, department stores, police and highway departments that want to discourage drunk driving, and funds for the homeless. Thanksgiving is a good time for Walk Your Talk cross-promotions among people who sell turkeys, food, and liquor, and nonprofits that feed hungry people on holidays.

Three potential Walk Your Talk cross-promotion partners whose cycles complement yours are:

1. _____

2. _____

3. _____

6. Organizations involved in the same kinds of activities or events that you are. Some businesses and organizations are natural partners, and will always be part of a team. These people can help one another — and have more fun working together — by giving referrals, coordinating their efforts, and cross-promoting. These events and activities might include:

- Weddings. Brides and grooms need florists, hair stylists, photographers, tuxedo rentals, dresses, caterers, musicians, limo rentals, hotel reservations, and a host of other services.

- Vacation and travel. This vast industry includes such potential Walk Your Talk cross-promotion partners as travel agents; AAA for maps, services, and information; clothing and outdoor equipment; auto rentals; luggage; banks for travelers' checks; and just about anyone else who might care to carve out a niche.

Three potential Walk Your Talk cross-promotion partners involved in similar activities or events to yours are:

1. _____

2. _____

3. _____

7. Organizations with which you already have a personal or professional connection. Ask yourself if there are potential partners among your friends, associates, current customers, vendors, or other acquaintances. Consider adding a Walk Your Talk cross-promotional dimension to these connections if it seems appropriate, valuable, and fun.

Also consider Walk Your Talk cross-promoting with businesses or organizations that you've always respected, liked, or admired — the Cancer Association, Meals on Wheels, a particularly imaginative boutique, or an anti-drug program.

There are ways to cross-promote with almost anyone, even if you do no more than putting up one another's cards or posters, and it feels good to form supportive alliances with groups whose work inspires you.

Three potential Walk Your Talk cross-promotion partners in this category are:

1. _____

2. _____

3. _____

As you begin choosing Walk Your Talk cross-promotion partners, give special consideration to two ideal teammates: local media and nonprofit organizations that support worthy causes.

IDEAL PARTNER #1: THE LOCAL MEDIA

Local media are extremely desirable Walk Your Talk cross-promoting partners because one of their functions is advertising and they reach vast numbers of people.

There are many kinds of local media — newspapers, magazines, television, and radio — and many different markets and subsegments within each of these broad categories. Your job is to pinpoint the one that best reaches the people you serve and focuses on your **mutual**

market. Then you have the foundation for a mutually beneficial partnership, and you aren't just going begging to the media to cash in on their huge audience.

Naturally, everybody wants to cross-promote with the media. You can make yourself the most attractive partner in one of three ways:

1. **Generate news.** This is the fuel that powers most media. If you are doing something genuinely newsworthy, they will be more interested in working with you.

2. **Lend your good name to the Walk Your Talk cross-promotion.** If you are a worthy cause or have some other claim to fame, the media can gain status in their audience's minds by associating with you.

3. **Come up with fun, creative Walk Your Talk cross-promotions that excite people** — and make them tune in or buy papers.
   When you launch a joint contest, award, or event with the media, give them added incentive to promote the venture as a public service by bringing in an uplifting nonprofit organization as your third partner. Whatever product or service you provide, joint campaigns with media for worthy causes (blood drives, food drives, collecting clothing for the homeless, etc.) mean high visibility and making friends in the community.

- Paul owned the largest pet store in town, and was one of the first people to visit the zoo's new baby elephant. He and Jan, the zoo director, went for coffee afterward and found themselves talking about the zoo's increasing need for private contributions and public awareness. They realized they had a mutual market — people who were interested in animals — and that they could work together to reach that market.
  They sat down with Marilyn, who owned a local radio station and was an animal lover herself, and came up with plans for a contest to name the new baby elephant. Paul offered a $250 gift certificate as the prize. The radio station donated about $2,000 worth of air time and got in return a reputation for supporting good causes, a general increase in listeners gener-

ated by a contest that was both fun and newsworthy, and a new group of listeners — people who were interested in animals. Through entry forms, Paul and Jan got access to the names and addresses of hundreds of animal lovers, people in their primary targeted audience. Both the pet store and the zoo got high visibility and traffic, the baby elephant got a name, and everyone who participated in or entered the contest had fun and felt good about themselves and their community.

- The heads of a local physician's group, a hospital, and the public health agency worked with local media to develop campaigns that spotlighted the dangers of lead paint, drugs, and lack of prenatal care. The media generated good will by providing a public service, the other agencies did their job better by distributing needed information more widely, all the Walk Your Talk cross-promoting partners gained a reputation for service to the community, and people were helped by what they did.

Chapter 9, "Make News: How to Access the Local Media," contains detailed suggestions for generating news, working with the media, and getting and keeping their attention.

IDEAL PARTNER #2: WORTHY CAUSES

Partnering with a worthy nonprofit organization or government agency gives you all the general advantages of Walk Your Talk cross-promotion, plus a high level of good will and much wider exposure because the media are more willing to cover and give public service time to these organizations.

You feel good, and your customers know that you are a responsible citizen who cares about the community. That influences where they take their business.

When deciding which worthy nonprofit organization or government agency to approach as a Walk Your Talk cross-promoting partner, first consider the people they reach. Do they speak to the same audience that you do? How will your target audience feel about that nonprofit? Think about the possible public relations impact — both positive and negative — and also ask yourself the following managerial questions:

- How long has the organization been in existence?

- Is it stable, reliable, and well managed? Can it show a full accounting of funds raised and spent?

- What percentage of the funds raised goes to the cause and what percentage to the management of the organization?

- How closely has the organization worked with business or profit-oriented partners in the past, and can you talk to previous partners about their participation?

- Does the organization have a good reputation with the public and the news media?

WHEN TO ADD OR SUBTRACT WALK YOUR TALK CROSS-PROMOTION PARTNERS

Keep thinking about new Walk Your Talk cross-promotion partners even when you already have one campaign underway. You may want to invite someone else to join you and your current partner, or you may think of a whole new way to cross-promote with a different set of people.

Add partners when a good idea strikes you and you feel that you can:

1. Begin a new Walk Your Talk cross-promotion without detracting from the one already underway

2. Bring a new partner into the current Walk Your Talk cross-promotion without upsetting the equilibrium among your present partners

Choose new partners the same way you chose your original ones — on the basis of mutual markets, the new people they can help you reach, and the good image, dynamic energy, or credibility they can bring to your cross-promotion. Remember to stay open to your current partners' ideas for new Walk Your Talk cross-promotional partners as well.

Occasionally, you may want to dissolve cross-promotion alliances. This may happen when:

1. People don't follow through on what they say they will do

2. Your joint efforts just don't seem to be working

3. Your partners act in inappropriate or unproductive ways that undermine your success, credibility, or image (being rude, doing shoddy work, offering an inferior product or service, taking ineffective or damaging actions without your approval, etc.)

SUMMARY

To find productive Walk Your Talk cross-promotion partners:

1. Define the people you want to reach in clear, specific terms.

2. Use the checklist in this chapter to find partners who can help you reach those people in positive, creative, mutually beneficial ways.

4

THE 14 STEPS TO SUCCESSFUL WALK YOUR TALK CROSS-PROMOTING

You've carefully defined your customers and identified some potential Walk Your Talk cross-promoting partners. Now what? How do you get from a list of possible partners to a successful Walk Your Talk cross-promotion?

The essence of Walk Your Talk cross-promotion is that you and your partner want to reach the same audience with a message that makes them want to use your products or services.

Turn your mutual markets into mutual benefits by following these simple, practical guidelines for approaching and working effectively with Walk Your Talk cross-promoting partners.

1. DEFINE YOUR MARKET IN THE MOST SPECIFIC TERMS YOU CAN. The exercises in Chapter 3 will help you do this. Set aside some time and write down your answers to those questions. Discover everything you can about the people you serve. Get specific, and then get **more** specific.

What do your customers want most — in their families, their friendships, their professions, in life? What do they want that you have? When do they want it? How can you best deliver it to them? How else do they spend their time and money? What do they think is important? What are their hot buttons, both positive and negative? What do they read, and when? Who influences them? Whom do they admire? What do they want that they don't have?

Who are your hidden or untapped markets? Who else might be interested in what you offer? What can you do to attract those people? Ask the same questions about the people in your hidden markets that you asked about the people you are now serving.

2. MAKE A LIST OF OTHER ORGANIZATIONS THAT SHARE THESE MARKETS. Next to each question or point, write the name of another organization that compliments yours and does not compete with you, but that shares those same markets.

3. WRITE DOWN WHAT YOU HAVE TO OFFER A PARTNER. After you've determined that you have a mutual market, the next step is to show your potential partners that they can benefit from working with you. Exactly what will they, or their customers, gain from an alliance with you? You might tell them about another Walk Your Talk cross-promotion you did that worked out well for all concerned, and show them the materials you used: flyers, posters, videos of events, etc. If you haven't cross-promoted before and don't have these materials available, you might make some sketches or mock-ups of your ideas.

You will bring your own special qualities and benefits to the partnership, but almost everyone can offer the following:

- A distribution channel. At the very least, you can get the word out about your partner's product or service to your own customers.

- Display space. You can display promotional material for your joint venture or for your partner on counter tops, walls, delivery trucks, and in windows.

- "Advertising" space. Ads can be printed on the backs of receipts, on posters in the store, on hangers, on flyers, or on the bags in which your customers take away their merchandise.

- Increased visibility for your partner's ads during your times of heavy traffic. Your traffic is probably heaviest at certain times of the day, month, or year — morning if you are a coffee shop or bakery, lunch hour if you're the Department of Motor Vehicles, the end of the month if you're the utility service office, the end of the summer if you're the health department that offers immunizations required for school. Your partners know that they can multiply their exposure by Walk Your Talk cross-promoting with you during these times.

- Donating your own products or services. These can be used as prizes or incentives for all kinds of contests, events, and promotions. The cost of donating your product or service is minimal and people experience first-hand what you do or offer.

- Becoming the "local expert" for media and other groups. If you become well known — even if only as the local gardening expert or the fix-it handyman on a local cable channel — you become a more valuable partner. Your expertise and fame, however modest, are capital that you bring to any Walk Your Talk cross-promotion.

- Your staff. Your staff will probably be an important part of the Walk Your Talk cross-promotion, and may volunteer to become even more involved with your partner's organization — especially if it is a worthwhile nonprofit or provides a unique or particularly interesting product or service.

- Space for an event. Is your store or office big enough to host an event? Do you have a parking lot that is big enough? Can your office be used as the site of an awards presentation for the winner, a few "officials," and two or three camera crews from the local TV stations? How can you make your physical space useful to your partner or the Walk Your Talk cross-promotion?

• Location. Do you have a heavy traffic location where people can hand out cards or coupons? Can you hand out joint promotional materials at your door or on the street in front of your place of business? Can you put a sandwich sign outside your store or office? How can you use your location to benefit your partner or your Walk Your Talk cross-promotion?

Think about the specific benefits that you bring to a partnership. What advantage does a partner gain by working with you? The people you approach about cross-promotion may not understand immediately what you have to offer them. You need to be very clear about what you bring to the table, so that you can remind them gently but clearly what you have to offer.

4. APPROACH YOUR STRONGEST POTENTIAL PARTNER FIRST. Your strongest potential partner is the one with whom you stand to reach the most people in your targeted audience, in the most effective ways. If you feel uncomfortable starting with that person, begin with someone you already know as a potential ally (a friend, an acquaintance from a civic group), or someone who would have a great deal to gain from working with you.

5. BE PREPARED; DO YOUR HOMEWORK. Spend some time preparing before you knock on anyone's door. Think about how to present yourself in the best possible light, and how to engage the other person's interest. Usually, this is a four-step process:

> Step 1. **Focus on what you have in common: a mutual market**. You share the same audience, or you wouldn't be interested in Walk Your Talk cross-promoting with this person. You may also share potential markets — people who might want to do business with both of you, but whom neither of you has reached yet. Most people want to attract more clients or customers to their organization, so you share that desire as well. As you talk, you may discover more that you have in common.

Step 2. **Focus on what the other person has to gain from working with you.** Talk about the general benefits of Walk Your Talk cross-promoting (see Chapter 2), and about the particular advantages of working with you. What can you bring to the partnership in terms of contacts, skills, personality, physical space, staff, expertise, customers, and products or services? Find out what else your potential partner might want to gain from Walk Your Talk cross-promoting, and see if you can provide it.

Step 3. **Focus on what you have to gain.** This may also suggest to your potential partner some other things that he or she may gain, and it keeps you from sounding too good to be true.

Step 4. **Then, and only then, focus on a specific promotion plan you have in mind.** Make sure you lay the groundwork with your first three steps, and only then start talking about specific promotions. Give your potential partner some idea of the kinds of things you have in mind — an event, a contest, mutual discounts, for instance — but don't lay everything out as a done deal. Let your partner help plan and develop the project so that he or she participates fully and "owns" the promotion as much as you do.

Your preparation may also involve role-playing for the first meeting with your potential partner, or drawing up some sample promotional materials to show him or her.

Adele's housewares shop was across the street from Sam's deli in an up-scale shopping area called "Sycamore Street." She knew they shared a market because she saw who went in and out of the deli, and literally watched people go back and forth between their two businesses every day. Adele knew there were ways to make that back-and-forth traffic even heavier, but was a bit shy about approaching Sam. She didn't know if he would welcome her, or her ideas.

To prepare for the meeting Adele did the following:

Step A. She wrote down exactly the market they shared: primarily upper-income women aged thirty to fifty who entertained regularly and were busy with volunteer or part-time work.

Step B. She made a list of what she could offer Sam: referrals from a similar customer base, promotional materials in her shop, a friendly staff who could be trained to mention the deli frequently, alluding to his deli on the weekly segments she did for a local television "home" show, and creating attractive displays in the deli using products from her shop.

Step C. She reviewed what she hoped to gain from working with Sam — more customers, more "Sycamore Street" community, a friend on the block — in order to combat her shyness about approaching him.

Step D. She came up with some promotional ideas to run by Sam.

When she felt ready, she called Sam and said, "Sam, this is Adele Smith from The Copper Pot across the street. I have something I'd like to talk over with you, and I wonder if I could buy you a cup of coffee at Sweet Tarts one day this week." Sam agreed to meet her at ten the next morning.

6. MEET TO SHARE YOUR GOALS AND DISCUSS YOUR RESPECTIVE NEEDS. Introduce yourself in a friendly, low-key way that isn't aggressive, pushy, or intimidating. You may be very excited about promotions you've considered for the two of you, but remember that your potential partners haven't had a chance to think this through. The advantages may not be clear to them at first, and they may be skeptical. Don't rush the process or suggest that you need them in order to implement your ideas. Take your time. Avoid doing anything to make them think that you are "selling" something or want to use them in any way.

Approach your potential partners as a supportive fellow member of whatever community you share (geographic, business, socially responsible, etc.) who recognizes that you have a mutual interest because you share the same market, who sees a genuine opportunity for mutual benefit, and who is offering them a chance to participate.

Talk about the shared markets and the general benefits of Walk Your Talk cross-promotion first, then move on to what your partner might gain. Next, talk about what you could gain from Walk Your Talk cross-promoting. Finally, suggest a few ideas for promotions that you might develop together. Work at a pace that is comfortable for both of you. Keep focused and moving forward without steamrolling your partners. Make sure that everybody participates in decisions.

The purpose of this initial contact is to introduce yourself, establish rapport, give them a general idea of the benefits of Walk Your Talk cross-promotion and a positive experience of you, start them thinking about what they have to gain, demonstrate specifically what you bring to the partnership, and schedule a meeting to discuss the possibility of Walk Your Talk cross-promoting in more detail.

Adele was early for her meeting with Sam, and rose to greet him. "Sam, I'm Adele. Thanks for coming. I didn't mean to sound mysterious, but I've been thinking about something that might be helpful to both of us. Let's get our coffee first." As they ordered and paid for their coffee and tarts, Adele made small talk to establish rapport. She asked Sam how business was, whether the recent rains had kept people away, and told him that she was getting addicted to his delicious potato salad. Sam beamed.

When they sat down, Adele began, "My brother-in-law was talking to me this weekend about something called Walk Your Talk cross-promoting, and I couldn't help thinking of you." She went on to describe the general benefits of Walk Your Talk cross-promoting, and suggested specific benefits to Sam whenever possible. "For instance," she said, "one thing we might do if you and I decided to cross-promote is put cards and flyers advertising the deli, and even your daily specials, in my shop. I've made a few sketches of the kinds of things we could use next to my cash register." She mentioned a few other benefits to Sam, and asked him what else he'd like to gain from working together. Then she moved on to the benefits that she would derive.

"It would be wonderful for me to meet some of your customers. If they're interested in your fine food, they're probably interested in presenting it attractively. I'd also like to make some closer connections with the Sycamore Street people, and working with you would be a start in that direction."

When she saw that Sam was in general agreement with what she was saying, and she could see his wheels starting to turn about the benefits he could gain by Walk Your Talk cross-promoting, she floated a few specific ideas. She was careful to leave room for his disagreement or input, but she wanted him to see that she had thought carefully about what they could do and was bringing some creativity to the venture.

"If you think it would work," she began, "I could make some displays for the deli — maybe place settings with brightly colored tablecloths and napkins, pretty glasses and flatware. You could put together a menu to display on the table, and every few days we could present a new table setting and menu."

Sam and Adele began with that promotion, which was a huge success, and went on to more elaborate events. The energy between the two businesses generated more customers for both of them, and other Sycamore Street merchants wanted to join in. Walk Your Talk cross-promoting sprang up everywhere and culminated in the Sycamore Street Fair a year later.

7. BRAINSTORM; CONSIDER THE BEST AND WORST THAT COULD HAPPEN. After your first meeting, get together to toss around ideas for Walk Your Talk cross-promotions. Consider the advantages and disadvantages of each, the best and worst that could happen.

These initial brainstorms may not become part of your final plan — many of them may not even be practical — but they may trigger other ideas that are brilliant. You may say something that prompts a flash of genius in your partners, and vice versa.

Sam and Adele's Walk Your Talk cross-promotion didn't come together overnight. They spent many weeks brainstorming and refining their plans — making such decisions as what kind of tone and style to set, whom to contact, and whether or not to do a joint mailing.

As you narrow your focus and start coming up with workable, mutually beneficial ideas, take each one and consider the best and worst that could happen if you tried it. Decide whether the potential gain is worth the possible risk.

8. DEVELOP A JOINT MARKETING PLAN. This is where you stop talking and start doing. You decide on actual plans and promotions, set dates, assign responsibilities, design materials, take them to the printer, prepare your staffs, and actually get underway. Chapter 6 contains questions and worksheets to help you develop a plan that meets both of your needs.

As you develop your joint marketing plan, make sure that everyone's investment is comparable and that you all stay focused on your goals. As a gesture of good will, you might volunteer to do the first part of the project.

9. START SMALL, AND GO SLOWLY. Begin with a simple, short-term Walk Your Talk cross-promotion that yields quick results: a joint mailing to both of your customer lists, flyers in one another's places of business, employees wearing T-shirts or badges with one another's logos, or one of the other suggestion in "10 Quick Starters" on page 18.

If you start too big — with a year-long campaign involving a pro basketball star to promote your sports shop, the high school basketball team, and the community youth club, for example — you may become overwhelmed, lose steam, get discouraged, and drop the whole idea of Walk Your Talk cross-promoting.

Set realistic goals that can be achieved, so that you build enthusiasm and good feelings among you and your partners. See what results your collaboration produces, and how well your styles work together. Where do you both feel most comfortable and successful? Where do you need to make adjustments?

Don't go too quickly. Take on only one new challenge at a time, and work at an easy pace. Finish a few simple promotions before advancing to more complex projects. Stay aware of how you feel about working together. If you start feeling uncomfortable, stop and explore what's happening before plunging into a new project.

Be prepared. You may need to change what you do or how you do it. Building a partnership is a bit like starting a relationship. Successful partners often say, "Each of us does 75% of the work."

10. OVERPLAN YOUR FIRST CROSS-PROMOTION. Remember that your first Walk Your Talk cross-promotion will be the most time-consuming. You're learning the ropes, and may be doing things you haven't done before: sending out press releases, calling reporters, or planning events.

It's important for your first Walk Your Talk cross-promotion to be successful, so that both you and your partners come away with good results and positive feelings. It's better to overplan than to underplan, better to spend a few extra hours or minutes on your promotion than to have it go awry.

11. REVIEW YOUR PROGRESS OFTEN, AND DEBRIEF WHEN THE FIRST PROJECT IS OVER. Keep tabs on yourself. Make a scrapbook of your media coverage. Compare sales or usage figures before, during, and after the Walk Your Talk cross-promotion.

Document your results as clearly and specifically as you can. This information not only keeps you focused on your needs, but can also help you interest future partners in Walk Your Talk cross-promotion.

Reviewing the promotion as you go along helps you adjust to changing circumstances and tailor your activities to suit current conditions. If a competitor starts to cut into your market or your partner's market, for instance, you can adjust to offset that problem.

When the entire Walk Your Talk cross-promotion is over, schedule a final debriefing with your partners. Write down exactly what results you produced together, and compare those results with your goals. Note where you could improve, and pat yourselves on the back for what you've achieved.

No project is perfect, and one or both of you may suggest doing things differently next time. Allow time for both of you to talk about what didn't work, as well as what did. Try to maintain a supportive environment for your debriefing, and don't take suggestions personally. If you are both able to express your views freely, you can learn from your experience and be even more effective next time.

12. ESTABLISH LONG-TERM GOALS AND PLANS. If you decide that Walk Your Talk cross-promoting benefits both of your organizations and you want to work together again, try collaborating on a long-term project that covers at least a year.

Before you begin, each of you should redefine your organization's long-term marketing goals. Decide what specific results you want to produce, and see if you can achieve those goals through a Walk Your Talk cross-promotion.

Take some time to brainstorm again, as you did when you started working together. When you've completed a successful Walk Your Talk cross-promotion, it's tempting to skip some of the initial steps and assume that you know everything about one another's organizations, goals, and working styles. This can lead to disaster. **Don't assume anything.** Follow the same careful steps that brought success last time.

13. BRANCH OUT. At some point, you may want to branch out and include other organizations in your Walk Your Talk cross-promotions. When you and your partner feel comfortable with one another and have formed at least a professional friendship, you become a strong sales team. You can approach new potential partners with a track record and show them specific results. You have documentation and testimonials that make Walk Your Talk cross-promoting credible to your potential partners. They can see what they might gain by teaming up with you.

Nevertheless, your ideas may seem unorthodox to them at first. Approach them in the same respectful manner and spirit of generosity that you approached your first partner. Talk about the general advantages of Walk Your Talk cross-promotion, and make sure that they understand the benefits without appearing to "sell" or push them. Then suggest a few ideas and see how they react.

14. KEEP AN EYE ON THE GROUP DYNAMICS AMONG YOUR WALK YOUR TALK CROSS-PROMOTING PARTNERS. Groups take on a life of their own, and working as a group can be more challenging than working alone or with only one partner. More personalities are involved, decision-making is more complex, everyone has individual as well as group goals, and you have to keep alert to the dynamics within your alliance.

As the original organizer, you may find yourself in the role of arbitrator if conflicts or difficulties arise. Working with the group may require more planning, more personal attention, and more diplomacy than working with only one partner. Some people may forget that your alliance is built on a spirit of genuine cooperation and push to "get theirs." Others may feel manipulated, and react either by getting angry or by withdrawing into resentment and ultimately leaving the group. You will get a closer look at everybody's strengths and weaknesses.

Aligning the group's goals and coordinating everybody's individual contributions can be more difficult than simply going off and doing the job by yourself, but the results of working with several partners can also be more rewarding and more far-reaching.

Use these fourteen steps as your guidelines whenever you want to include more partners in a current Walk Your Talk cross-promotion or begin a new promotion with new partners. They will keep you focused on your goals and sensitive to your own and others' needs. Ultimately, they will result in reaching more people, more effectively, at less cost — and at the same time building a sense of cooperation, respect, and trust with your partners and the entire community.

SUMMARY

1. Approach potential partners respectfully, emphasizing:

- Your shared markets

- Specific benefits to them of working with you

- Benefits to you

- Possible Walk Your Talk cross-promotions

2. Develop a marketing plan that focuses on your mutual goals. Start small, record results, check your progress, and expand as you feel comfortable with one another and with Walk Your Talk cross-promoting.

3. Branch out to include new partners and larger projects, but be alert to the dynamics of the bigger group.

CHAPTER 5

BREAKING INTO
THE BIG LEAGUES

You can play in the big leagues of Walk Your Talk cross-promotion even if you are a tiny retailer (or a small local branch of a huge business) with two employees, a committee-of-one running the clothing drive at your nonprofit church, or the lowliest municipal agency in town.

The big leagues are about quality, not size — quality in the product or service you provide, and in the way you promote it. Walk Your Talk cross-promotion is an opportunity to enrich the quality of what you do and how you do it. It expands your horizons in many ways:

1. You have a clearer sense of who your customers are and how you can serve them better.

2. You work with a partner, so you are supporting others and building a sense of community.

3. You speak to more people, and deliver a message that you've recently reviewed and improved.

Playing in the big leagues simply means being willing to expand your ideas about what is possible and work with others in a spirit of mutual respect and appreciation.

NINE KEYS TO BREAKING INTO THE BIG LEAGUES

These nine keys will keep you on track as you expand your vision, look for new ways to cross-promote your product or service, and move to new levels of quality in both your product and your promotion:

1. FOCUS ON YOUR CUSTOMERS' NEEDS. Speak to your customers' values and interests, rather than to why they should buy what you are selling. If you let your business become product-driven, rather than customer-driven, you may discover what the Ford Motor Company discovered: they had plenty of factories to make Edsels, but no customers to buy them.

If you manage a health club, for instance, you need to keep current with all the latest health, exercise, sports, and weight-control trends — but you also need to keep in touch with your customers about what **they** want and need today. What effect does the economy have on how much they use your facilities, and on whether they extend their memberships or buy workout clothes and equipment in the small shop on your premises? What can you do to make it easier for them to use your services? Would they appreciate incentive deals, frequent-user discounts, package plans for families or companies? Ask your clients what they want, and what you could be doing better.

If you start Walk Your Talk cross-promoting with a health food store, you'll need to ask these questions again from a Walk Your Talk cross-promotional point of view. How can you mix and match products, services, and incentives to serve both your customers and the health food customers better? How can you use that doubled service to draw new customers? People who might not join your club or shop regularly at the health food store might have a positive first experience of both through a joint "Eat Right/Exercise Right" promotion that included:

- A free initial visit and tour of your facilities upon presentation of a coupon available in the paper and the health food store

- Reciprocal discounts that let "frequent buyers" at the store join your club at a reduced rate, and coupons for values at the health food store available in your club

• Joint educational programs free to the public

• Reciprocal staff education, so that your employees know more about nutrition and the health food store's employees know more about the benefits of exercise — and the two staffs can refer people back and forth

Walk Your Talk cross-promotion keeps you thinking in terms of your customers, because mutual markets are the basis of everything you do.

2. FIND YOUR NICHE. "Niche marketing" means targeting a narrower audience and establishing your particular niche in that market — the specific group of people you serve, and the unique way you serve them. The most successful marketers of the 1990s have concentrated on developing closer relationships with specific groups of customers, and establishing a lasting dialogue with them.

Target the right audience and speak directly to those people — when and where they are most likely to listen. Proctor and Gamble uses more shopping cart ads, because their products are found in grocery stores. Tiremaker B.F. Goodrich spends nearly a third of its marketing budget on events like auto races. Burger King now spends half of its ad budget on local tie-ins to build traffic in its franchises.

"A niche market is oriented first to people; second to product; third to place; and finally to occasion," according to Brian G. Harron of Harron Enterprises in Phoenix. (*Restaurant Business*, May 1, 1986) "Identify the heaviest potential customers/consumers. `Everybody' is not your customer, from a marketing standpoint."

"If you try to please everybody, you don't get anybody's market," says Danny O'Malia of O'Malia Food Markets in Indianapolis.

One of the best and most common ways to target a specific market is by setting up a "club." Barbie and Hot Wheels aren't the only companies that have clubs for "tweens" (seven to twelve years old). They are joined by Kraft, Gitano, the Keebler Elves, Kool Aid, Household Bank, Delta Airlines, Lego blocks, Toys "R" Us, Fox Broadcasting, Burger King, and Family Circle. Some charge a fee, and most issue a membership card and a bag of small complimentary items like stenciled pads, pencils, and calendars, which are themselves promotional materials. Some clubs have been particularly successful:

- More than one million children have joined the Burger King Kids' Club since 1990, when it was launched to lure young customers away from McDonald's, which for the past eight years had dominated the children's market, the fastest growing segment of the fast food business. Kids have taken home Lickety Splits (toys shaped like burgers and fries), Teenage Mutant Ninja Turtle character badges, and Beetlejuice figurines with kid club meals — and Burger King is "their" place.

- Since the Disney Channel revamped Mickey's club in 1990, thirty thousand tweens spent $12.95 each for a watch and magazine about the New Mickey Mouse Club Show, which makes them even more loyal fans.

- For every dollar that little Household Bank Banker Bear Savings Club members deposit, they receive a Banker Bear Buck redeemable for teddy bears, dinosaurs, radios, and other loot.

Many clubs were designed to sell merchandise related to the core product — Barbie clothes and Batman secret decoder rings, for instance — but others were set up as independent profit streams, using the company's name and good will to sell unrelated goods.

"Clubs for tweens establish an ongoing involvement that lets a company recapture the tween audience again and again," according to Dale Wallenius, publisher of *The Marketing to Kids Report*.

When you cross-promote, you have to be particularly conscious of what your niche is and how you and your partner are reaching it.

3. MARKET-IT-YOURSELF. The trend toward do-it-yourself, in-house marketing is gaining momentum as businesses discover that people respond best to direct, immediate, personal messages — preferably with local tie-ins. The new dictum is: If you want people to care about you and your product, show that you care about **them**.

Traditional advertising still has a role to play in Walk Your Talk cross-promotion and some of it is excellent — but messages that come directly from you to your customers can be even more effective, especially if your ad budget is small or if you are targeting a narrow audience.

You may want to combine the best of both worlds, and hire a local advertising agency that can bring its professional skills to bear on your

Walk Your Talk cross-promotion but also work with you to maintain an intimate, local "feel" — or you may want to hire a local graphic designer to create promotional materials: unusual receipts, promotional postcards, or special offer coupons.

Experts are singing the praises of marketing-it-yourself because:

- It is more cost-effective.

- It is more credible. Customers are more loyal to "real people" who are saying something that appears genuine than they are to slick ads.

- It is tied more closely to the community. You can capitalize on your specific knowledge about the place you live, and stress your ties with customers.

- You don't get dependent on advertising, and become afraid to stop using it even when you can't afford it.

To market-it-yourself effectively, you have to know your community as well as you do your customers. What are the two largest high schools in town? Can you name three grammar schools? Five churches? Six nonprofit organizations? Thirty retail merchants? Three dry cleaners? Four movie theaters? Two bowling alleys? Two health clubs?

4. GET ON THE SOCIALLY RESPONSIBLE BANDWAGON.
The true heroes of today's marketing arena are socially responsible businesses that contribute to their communities by teaming up with worthy environmental, health, or social causes.

They are doing good in the world, and getting credit for it. People are more likely to use their product or service because by supporting these socially responsible organizations, they feel that they, too, are somehow doing good. If they have $5, $50, or $500 to spend on comparable products at either a socially responsible business or a business that is just looking after its own interest, most people will choose the organization that is helping others.

Working with uplifting causes not only makes you feel good, it helps your bottom line. You become known as a "responsible adult" organization, someone who understands the importance of contributing to others and building community. Many businesses are reaping the moral and financial rewards of being one of the "big kids":

- "Corporate community involvement programs add value to the workplace, the industry, and the community," says Richard Smith, Senior Vice President of Administration for Days Inn of America, which has a policy of hiring homeless people. "We hire and train them as national reservations and sales agents for our reservation centers in Atlanta and Knoxville . . . We simply want to hire employable people who, in this case, happen to be homeless. We don't have to recruit these people actively. They are referred to us through various area shelters." The publicity surrounding this project has created enormous good will.

- After the firestorm that leveled three thousand dwellings in Oakland, California, a group of Bay Area photographers shot and processed about three hundred family portraits for people who lost decades of photographs in the blaze. You can bet that these fire victims, and people who read about the project in local and national media, will choose one of those photographers the next time they have a wedding or family reunion.

- Many banks and credit card companies have developed "affinity cards" and checks that cross-promote such worthy causes as Sierra Club, National Child Safety Council, Greenpeace, Vietnam Veterans of America, National Organization for Women, and National Audubon Society. Each time you use the card or order checks, the group receives a donation — and spreads its message.

- Even the government is getting into the act, with the Departments of Defense and Education cross-promoting to help former military personnel find jobs in the post-Cold War era. "In the past few years, several colleges have developed programs to certify ex-military personnel for teaching jobs. Since June, nearly eleven thousand soldiers have called army hotlines that give information about teaching careers," according to *USA Today*.

5. SELL THE REAL BENEFITS OF YOUR PRODUCT, NOT JUST THE BELLS AND WHISTLES. People want quality. If your product or service is good, and people are reminded that it is good, they will come back again and again. Focus on what you do best, and stress the genuine benefits of using your product or service.

When ConAgra brought out Healthy Choice, a line of low-fat, health-oriented frozen entrees, it did not rely on old marketing methods. Five years earlier, the promotion would have stressed, "mass, mass, mass, cheap, cheap, cheap," says Karen Murray, Associate Media Director on the account for the Campbell-Mithun-Esty agency in Minneapolis. Instead, Healthy Choice emphasized its one unique quality — being genuinely healthy and low fat — and made that the foundation of all its marketing. Health-consciousness was even the basis of its Walk Your Talk cross-promotions. A health magazine helped set up promotions in health clubs in return for Healthy Choice placing an ad.

Healthy Choice could have based its promotion on attractive packaging and interesting food combinations, but chose to emphasize its genuine benefits to consumers. The strategy worked.

6. FOCUS ON YOUR PRODUCT OR SERVICE'S DISTINGUISHING CHARACTERISTICS. What one thing makes your product or service absolutely unique? What can you do to **create** one unique quality that distinguishes your organization from all others in the field?

Danny O'Malia's Food Market in Indianapolis faced stiff competition until he started focusing on his distinguishing characteristic: specialty and ethnic fruits and vegetables that no one else in his area stocked. O'Malia could have used this unique characteristic to connect with Walk Your Talk cross-promotion partners as well: local gourmet groups and publications, ethnic organizations, health clubs and organizations, and vegetarian groups.

When you focus on your best points and unique characteristics, marketing becomes almost fail-safe — and emphasizing your areas of expertise or excellence should also suggest natural Walk Your Talk cross-promotion partners.

Colgate recently defied convention by joining competitor Warner-Lambert Co. in a novel promotion: Buy a tube of Colgate toothpaste and a bottle of Warner-Lambert's Listerine mouthwash, and get a ($1.99 value) Colgate toothbrush free. This Walk Your Talk cross-promotion earned one of the highest display-exposure levels ever, says

Colgate Promotion Director Keith Jones. It also made a nationwide sampling campaign for the toothbrush unnecessary. Estimated savings: $15 million.

Use marketing strategies that have been tested and proven by large national companies, like the Colgate-Listerine cross-promotion, and adapt them to your scale and needs. What organization in your area would be a good partner for this type of Walk Your Talk cross-promotion?

7. BE PREPARED FOR CUSTOMERS' OBJECTIONS — AND LISTEN WHEN THEY SPEAK. Successful salespeople will tell you that you can't sell anything if you aren't prepared to listen to your potential customers' problems and concerns about your product or service. Dealing with objections is an essential part of any sales training or experience. It's also a good way to get suggestions for improving your product and how you present it.

When people are allowed to voice their objections, and feel heard, then they can let go of those concerns and often become even more loyal. When they can't talk about what's bothering them, or they don't feel heard, they cling to those objections for dear life. They may simply go away and complain about you to their friends, so that you lose both their business and their friends' business.

Each person who uses your product or service wants to feel like your most important customer. Welcome their input, and listen to what they say. Never make excuses like "The computer did it." Use what they tell you to improve both your product or service, and the way you market and cross-promote it. Find out what they like and don't like. Ask regular customers what brings them back. Ask people who haven't been in lately what keeps them away. You may need to make some changes, but you will upgrade customer satisfaction — and that means more customers.

Input from customers can actually prompt productive new alliances:

- The local Planned Parenthood office received complaints that their 9–5 hours weren't convenient for working women, and arranged to stay open until 8 PM using volunteers from the local AIDS organization, which distributed their own information as well.

- Parents complained that their children weren't receiving enough information about nutrition in local grammar schools. The school board responded by inviting various health organizations and the local dietitians' association to speak in classes on a regular basis, a move that pleased and benefited everyone. Health food stores also sent representatives, and got valuable exposure with a young audience.

8. BE A GENUINE RESOURCE TO CLIENTS. <u>Let customers know that you are there to serve them</u>, not just to sell to them. Give them valuable information that costs you little or nothing, and keeps them coming back:

- Pillsbury sends newsletters to everyone who has contacted the company about products.

- Green Giant vegetable customers get a letter packed with recipes and nutritional information, as well as advertising for new products.

Walk Your Talk cross-promoting is a way to offer your customers even more information and become a better resource:

- A sports store teamed up with the local group of orthopedic physicians to develop a tip sheet on avoiding athletic injuries. The store became a medical resource, and customers had in hand a list of orthopedists in case they got injured anyway.

- A nearby maternity wear shop watched the sport store's success and began a similar promotion on prenatal care with the local OB-GYNs.

- The fire department distributed "Fourth of July Safety Tips" at a fast food outlet where children and teens gathered, and warnings about Christmas decoration hazards at the hardware store where many of them were purchased. Information went directly to the people who needed it most — and both the fast food outlet and the hardware store became genuine sources of information.

9. DON'T FORGET THE TIE-BREAKERS: TIRELESS SERVICE AND VALUE-ADDED ELEMENTS. In today's stressed and hurried world, quality human contact gives you an incalculable advantage. All things being equal between you and your competitors, people will go where they feel best.

The more service you provide, and the more grace with which you and your employees provide it, the better your customers feel. Tireless service can bring and keep more customers than millions of dollars in advertising. Make sure your employees understand the value of serving customers well, and offer them incentives to do so.

Find out what kinds of service are most important to your customers — additional business hours, deliveries, more staff, etc. — and give them whatever you can.

As always, design the special service to suit your target group. If you target senior citizens, for instance, remember that they don't like to be rushed. They prefer familiar employees, especially ones who will look at their grandchildren's pictures with them. Danny O'Malia distinguished his food store to that group by providing a sitting area where customers could rest, and "box boys" to carry shopping bags to the parking lot.

The other way to break a tie between you and your competitors is to offer your customers more for their money: discounts, "frequent-buyer" coupons, samples, gifts, or other incentives. Ask your customers which incentives they prefer, and give them what they want.

What special services and value-added elements are best suited to the group you want to target?

MICKEY'S TEN COMMANDMENTS

Disney uses "Mickey's Ten Commandments" to market all Disney products, and they have resulted in some of the most successful promotions in history.

Sit down with your partner and decide how you can apply these principles to your local Walk Your Talk cross-promotions:

1. Know your audience. Start with the worksheets in this book, and repeat the exercises at least once every six months to keep current.

2. Wear your guests' shoes. Walt Disney made many improvements to the original Disneyland after walking around as if he were visiting for the first time.

3. Organize the flow of people and ideas. A message should flow naturally, like a story — with a beginning, middle, and end.

4. Create a weenie, or a visual magnet to draw people in. This can be your "signature," or simply a large sign in an eye-catching color.

5. Communicate with visual literacy. Scale and color reinforce themes, sustain interest, and define your customers' comfort level. If you want people to relax in your place of business, don't paint the walls red or orange. If you want people to feel comfortable, intimate and open, don't put them in a large room with twenty-foot ceilings and no furniture.

6. Keep it simple. Avoid overloading your customers' minds or senses. Keep the focus on your product or service; don't distract them with a lot of visual or audio clutter. Instead, create easy-to-internalize turn-ons: simple signs, solid colors, one large "signature" display.

7. Tell one story at a time. Don't confuse people with mixed messages, metaphors, or styles — or give them too many messages at one time.

8. Avoid contradictions; maintain identity. Keep the message and themes simple and consistent.

9. Ounce of treatment; ton of treat. Make it fun for people to visit your place of business, so that they enjoy their time with you and want to come back. At Disney restaurants, waiters and waitresses are called Mom and Pop and ask if you've eaten your vegetables.

10. Keep it up. Repeat your message — over and over again.

Moving into the big leagues is simple when you concentrate on the quality of your product or service, give your customers what they want, market according to the guidelines in this chapter, and create Walk Your Talk cross-promotions that benefit both you and your partners.

SUMMARY

Remember "Mickey's Ten Commandments" and these nine guidelines for moving into the big leagues:

1. Focus on your customers' needs.

2. Find your niche.

3. Market-it-yourself.

4. Get on the socially responsible bandwagon.

5. Sell the real benefits of your product, not just the bells and whistles.

6. Focus on your product or service's distinguishing characteristics.

7. Be prepared for customers' objections — and listen when they speak.

8. Be a genuine resource to clients.

9. Don't forget the tie-breakers: tireless service and value-added elements.

6

HOW TO DEVELOP A JOINT MARKETING PLAN

You've mastered the basics of this new approach to Walk Your Talk cross-promoting: mutual markets, mutual benefits, mutual concerns, and mutual success. Now it's time to put those ideas into practice and come up with an action plan.

As you complete the worksheets in this chapter, let these words guide every decision you make:

> **Marketing has one goal:** to reach the maximum number of current and potential customers, most often, for the lowest possible cost, with a message that clearly describes the most important benefits of using your products or services.

THE FIVE Ws: WHO, WHAT, WHEN, WHERE, AND WHY

To keep your marketing plan focused and on target, borrow a technique from news reporters. Concentrate on the five Ws: Who, What, When, Where, and Why.

WHO are your customers? You've already done some of this research. Now you will look more closely at how these people make decisions about which product or service to use, and what you can do to keep old customers and attract new ones.

WHAT specific actions will you take to reach them most effectively? The worksheets in this chapter will help you generate ideas for getting your message out to people who want to use your product or service.

WHEN will you take these steps? You and your partners will decide exactly when your Walk Your Talk cross-promotion will be most effective, and work out a schedule so that everything gets done and nobody goes crazy.

WHERE are your potential customers likely to hear your message? You'll discover and target the specific media that influence them most strongly.

WHY are you doing all this in the first place? Not to have a bad time, distract from your business, or get crazy. You are marketing your product or service so that more people will know about it and use it.

Whenever you feel bogged down, return to the five Ws. Bottom line, a marketing plan just means deciding WHO, WHAT, WHEN, WHERE, and WHY.

BECOME YOUR OWN EXPERT

You and your partner understand the people you serve, your organizations, and your community better than anyone. Your best ideas for Walk Your Talk cross-promotions will occur spontaneously as you talk about your customers and organizations. You are the experts, the most effective architects and engineers of a joint marketing plan to serve your organizations.

Developing your own promotions puts you in good company. *INC.* magazine described this national trend in an article titled "Do-It-Yourself Marketing: How Smart Companies are Selling More and Spending Less" (November 1991):

"We've talked to dozens of [innovative start-up] companies recently, some old, some new, some with revenues of less than a million, some with revenues in the tens of millions. They all have one thing in common: they're doing more of their own marketing in-house and they're liking it better."

The article notes that five words come up repeatedly as people explain why they like doing their own marketing:

"**Control**: In this chaotic economy, managers want as much control as possible over all phases of their operations . . .

"**Flexibility**: As competition keeps apace, chief executives have to be able to move quickly and aggressively, and they have a much better chance at that when the work is done inside their companies . . .

"**Clutter**: To get a product or service noticed these days, a company has to be innovative to get through the clutter of advertisements and direct mail . . .

"**Quality**: To a person, those we talked with thought the quality of work done in-house was far superior to that farmed out. The common refrain ran, 'No one knows our company like we do' . . .

"**Savings**: For the most part, managers reported significant cost savings by doing all or part of their own marketing . . .

"Overall, the companies we've been talking with are evangelical about their do-it-yourself approach to marketing. And one thing's for certain: it's hard to argue with the results."

You have the answers, and the following worksheets will give you the right questions.

JOINT MARKETING
PLAN WORKSHEETS

The most important part of developing your marketing plan is collecting information to target your potential customers quickly, directly, and powerfully. That information divides into six categories, which are the focus of the questions in this chapter:

Defining your customers

Identifying how they get their information

Pinpointing your competition

Recognizing how you can improve what you give customers

Communicating your message effectively

Discovering what you can do to draw more clients or customers

If you rush into a Walk Your Talk cross-promotion without giving careful consideration to each of these items, you may be wasting time, energy, and money. Answer these questions thoroughly, preferably in writing. They may suggest completely new ideas about how to present your product or service. You may find more creative ways to accomplish what you want, and discover new marketing vistas that you never would have considered.

You and your Walk Your Talk cross-promoting partners can each answer these questions individually so that you are clear on your own marketing goals, then come together and answer them as a team to develop your joint marketing plan. You may want to take a month or two to research some of the answers. Use the techniques in Chapter 3 to collect information from or about current customers or clients.

Take a deep breath, and jump in.

1. Describe your organizations and the main products or services they provide.

Partner A: _____

_____

Partner B: _____

_____

2. Who are the customers you share? Be specific.

General Profile: _____

_____

Age: _____

Sex: _____

Occupation: _____

Income: _____

Geography: _____

Interests: _____

Values: _____

Concerns: _____

3. When you ask the people who buy your kind of products or services, "What are the top three criteria you use in making your selection?" they say:

1. _____

2. _____

3. _____

4. When you ask these people where they first heard of you, they say:

1. _____

2. _____

3. _____

5. What are you doing to encourage current customers to keep coming back? Do your employees remember the names of regular customers? Do you? Do customers feel that they are served promptly by knowledgeable people? Every customer should hear these words: "Thank you," "I'm glad you came in; please come back again," "If you have any questions, please call."

Is there a conspicuous sign in your place of business that reinforces these important messages with phrases like: "Come back soon," "We value your business," "Is there a way we could serve you better?"

Do you offer "frequent-buyer" discounts for regular customers? Do you make it easy, convenient, and profitable for customers to buy more from you? Do you give them a reason to tell their friends about your product or service — and to keep coming back?

List the ways in which you honor your current customers:

1. _____

2. _____

3. _____

4. _____

6. List five more ways you could encourage current customers to come back or buy more. Remember to take advantage of your partnership. Now you have twice as much to offer customers. Consider discounts or coupons for one another's products or services.

1. _____

2. _____

3. _____

4. _____

5. _____

7. How can you get your current customers to want more of your products, or need more of your services? Many companies, including California Cosmetics, report that 10% of their business comes from current customers who buy more.

1. _____

2. _____

3. _____

8. Who are the customers you would both like to attract, but do not now have?

1. _____

2. _____

3. _____

4. _____

5. _____

9. What can you offer these people?

New Customer   Benefits We Can Offer

_____   _____

_____   _____

_____   _____

_____   _____

_____   _____

10. Where do your potential customers get their information?

_____

_____

11. How do they decide which product or service to use?

_____

_____

12. Who else shares these customers?

_____

_____

13. How can you attract more first-time users or customers? You and your partner will both draw new people through your Walk Your Talk cross-promotion, but you can also "trade" customers by giving reciprocal "first-time" discounts and coaching your staffs on how to generate enthusiasm for the other organization. What other ways can you attract first-time customers?

1. _____

2. _____

3. _____

4. _____

5. _____

14. What are some of your joint "missed markets?" These are potential customers whom you may not have recognized as part of your market. List five of your "missed markets," people who might be interested in your products or services, but who have not yet connected with you.

1. _____

2. _____

3. _____

4. _____

5. _____

15. What are the strongest benefits of your products or services?

_____

_____

16. What are the particular details, qualities, or elements of your products or services that you think are most important to your customers?

_____

_____

17. How can you improve your products or services? Your product or service should be the best it can be so that you feel good about promoting it.

_____

_____

18. Who are your strongest competitors? Rank them in order:

1. _____

2. _____

3. _____

19. How are you positioned against this competition? In what ways are your products or services better, worse, the same as, or different from those of your competition? Use the same words you believe your prospective customers would use.

Competitor	Your product vs. theirs
_____	_____
_____	_____
_____	_____

20. How can you improve your competitive position? What could you change in order to look better next to your competition, or to stand out more clearly in the public's mind? List the specific ways you could modify your products or services — or the ways you offer them — to make them more appealing to potential customers.

1. _____

2. _____

3. _____

21. What is the primary joint message you want to communicate?

_____

_____

22. How is this message aligned with your customers' needs, values, and interests? Your goal is not to tell customers why you believe they should buy your product, but to understand **their** interests and speak to their concerns.

Benefit in Message	Customer's Concern
_____	_____
_____	_____
_____	_____

23. How frequently do you want your potential customers to hear this message?

_____

_____

24. How can you make your message more vivid? Build your message around:

- The reasons that people use your products or services

- How you want to be positioned in the minds of your prospects

Convey the benefits in words that are important — to your customers, not necessarily to you. What is your most impressive consumer benefit? Write it so that it can be said or read in sixty seconds or less.

_____

_____

25. What "extras" can you provide to distinguish your organizations from others and add value to your products or services (convenient hours, guarantees, speed of delivery, etc.)?

1. _____

2. _____

3. _____

26. What "signature" distinguishes your Walk Your Talk cross-promotion and sets it apart from all others? People remember "signatures": a salesman who always wears a bow tie, an executive who keeps a fresh rose on her desk every day, the furniture dealer who dresses in funny clothes for TV ads, a car wash with an enormous illuminated sign of an elephant spraying water from its trunk, or some other distinctive logo.

Your signature should be something that people not only remember, but talk about with their friends, colleagues and neighbors. Get feedback from your customers and employees about your signature's impact and how well people remember it. If you don't already have a signature, jot down some ideas here:

My current signature is: _____

Some new ideas for a signature are: _____

_____

27. What one thing can you do to make your joint campaign absolutely unforgettable?

_____

_____

28. What can you do to get honest feedback from clients or customers about your joint campaign? You might consider a small gift or handout if they complete a questionnaire, or coupons for themselves or their friends.

1. _____

2. _____

3. _____

4. _____

These questions should give you a good idea of who your customers are, how they get their information, what you can do to make your organization more attractive to them, how to communicate your message effectively, and how you can involve more people in your enterprise.

BRAINSTORMING

When you've completed these worksheets, brainstorm with your partner about the information you've collected, and what kinds of Walk Your Talk cross-promotions it suggests.

Remember, there are three ways to generate more business for your organizations:

1. Find new customers.

2. Get your current customers to use your product or service more often.

3. Get customers to buy or use more on each visit.

Keep all three in mind as you talk about possible Walk Your Talk cross-promotions and start to narrow your focus down to one or two. There is no right way to cross-promote, and no right plan for everyone. What works for one partnership may backfire for another. Go with the ideas that feel right to you and your partner.

Approach your promotion with a positive and enthusiastic attitude. Think of it as a party, an opportunity for people to participate with you and enjoy your product or service. Don't let fear slow you down.

In case you are having trouble getting started, here is a list of basic, proven ways to cross-promote:

- Billboards and marquees

- Signs and flyers

- TV and radio advertising, talk shows, public service announcements, news, and features — don't forget cable and PBS

- Newspaper news, feature, and specialty sections

- Local magazine news and features

- Local "advertiser" freebies

- Your own newsletter

- Logos on bags, receipts, employee clothing

- Giveaways

- Drawings and contests

- Discounts, coupons, and value-added cards for "frequent buyers," first-time users, one another's customers, and friends of employees

- Prizes or additional discounts for customers who spend $100, $250, or $500 a month at your store

- Events

- Speeches

- Passing out one another's flyers, business cards, coupons, promotional materials, samples

- Demonstrations of your products or services in one another's places of business

- Team up with organizations that do large mailings or billings — your local department store, for example — and have them include a 10% discount card for your business in their next mailing

Part II of this book describes other types of Walk Your Talk cross-promotions. As you read, think about how each might apply to you and your partner.

PUTTING IT ON PAPER

You've done your homework, gathered information, and brainstormed about ideas. Now it's time to make some decisions.

Putting your plan on paper makes it more concrete and real. Don't skip this important step; it is your statement of intention and purpose, the cornerstone to which you can return for strength and inspiration.

Writing your marketing plan is a simple three-step process, no matter how simple or complex your cross-promotion:

1. **Choose a Walk Your Talk cross-promotion activity.** Read over your worksheets again. Think about your answers. Discuss them with friends, associates, and your partner. Make a list of the five best possible actions.

1. _____

2. _____

3. _____

4. _____

5. _____

Now select one that you and your partner find exciting, and that you believe will produce the results you want.

2. Schedule activities and assign responsibilities. Most Walk Your Talk cross-promotions involve many small actions or activities — everything from designing flyers and getting them printed to hiring a concert hall for your event. Each small activity needs a completion date, and a person who is in charge.

Break down your Walk Your Talk cross-promotion into its smallest parts, put someone in charge of each activity, and assign it a completion date:

Action	Date	Person in Charge

3. Schedule debriefings. How will you know if you're successful? Hold debriefings with your key people at least once every month, more frequently if this is your first Walk Your Talk cross-promotion or the first time you've worked with this partner. At these meetings, talk about what is happening, what is working, and what is not working. This way, you find out early on if there is trouble or people having difficulty with their assignments. Debriefings are also a chance to support one another, build enthusiasm, and invite creative input.

When the Walk Your Talk cross-promotion is complete, you should all sit down for a final debriefing. Set aside this time to discuss both what went well and what could be improved, and to acknowledge everyone's efforts and your success.

Date	Debrief With	To Discuss

Remember, you don't always double your volume the first time out. Developing successful marketing programs sometimes involves trial and error. Congratulate yourself for having the courage to take a risk, and for the results you've achieved.

SUMMARY

The most important part of any joint marketing plan is doing your homework. You target your market most quickly, efficiently, effectively, and directly when you know:

- Who your customers are

- Where they get their information

- Who your competition is

- How you can improve your product or service

- What your message is and how to communicate it so that it reaches your target market most effectively

- What you can do to draw more customers

When you are armed with this information, designing your marketing plan is a simple three-step process:

1. Choose a Walk Your Talk cross-promotion activity.

2. Schedule activities and assign responsibilities.

3. Schedule debriefings.

PART TWO

PRACTICAL
WALK YOUR TALK
CROSS-PROMOTIONAL
IDEAS

CHAPTER 7

JOIN AMERICA'S NEW PROMOTIONAL DREAM TEAM

Partnerships between generous corporations and worthy nonprofit causes can help everybody — if they are done carefully and responsibly. Consider "adopting" an uplifting nonprofit cause if you are a business, or a business if you are an uplifting cause.

WIN-WIN-WIN

We've already touched on the triple benefit of businesses teaming up with worthy nonprofit organizations and government agencies: you **feel** good, you **do** good, and people associate you with the good work done by the cause. It's a way to be socially responsible, and at the same time polish your image.

TEAMING UP

When you choose a cause that interests or prompts positive emotional reactions in your specific audience, the benefits multiply. A company that makes binoculars might team up with the Audubon Society, an outdoor outfitter with the Sierra Club, or a pet store with the Society for the Prevention of Cruelty to Animals. Again, you're benefiting from the power of mutual markets — and so is the worthy cause.

You create advertising that doesn't look like advertising, but that generates exposure, good will, and new customers.

You also ride the wave of the future in American business. In *The Popcorn Report: Faith Popcorn on the Future of Your Company, Your World, Your Life* (Doubleday/Currency, 1991), America's top forecaster lists among the ten leading trends for the 1990s: "SOS (Save Our Society)." SOS translates into more businesses becoming socially responsible — partly from good intentions, partly to create good will that becomes good business — plus more volunteerism, and consumers refusing to buy products that pollute the environment or damage people's lives.

If you are a uplifting nonprofit cause, the obvious benefit of Walk Your Talk cross-promoting with business is that you have access to more money and other resources to promote your service. You also tap into their audience, which should be the same as yours. You sidestep the one potential drawback of teaming up with business — getting "bought off" and treated like a "poor relation" — because your part-ners are just as interested in reaching your people as you are in reach-ing theirs. Together, you can draw more of those same kinds of people to both of your organizations.

To make doubly sure that the balance of power is equal, be careful about the partners you choose. Both parties should know exactly what each will give and get *before* they start working together. When a spirit of generosity and equality surrounds these partnerships, everybody wins and nobody feels used.

In the fall of 1987, American Express and Waldenbooks sent 10¢ from every card-based transaction to Reading is Fundamental (RIF), a motivational program for literacy aimed at adults. For every new card application form that came from a Waldenbooks check-out rack, American Express sent $2 to RIF.

What was the benefit to American Express and Waldenbooks? They reached the kinds of people who support and hear news about literacy programs — *readers*, exactly the people in their market.

This new win-win-win approach to Walk Your Talk cross-promoting between business and nonprofit organizations is spelled out in "The Walk Your Talk Cross-promotion Partners' Bill of Rights" at the end of this chapter.

TESTIMONIALS YOU CANNOT BUY

Teaming up with "do-gooder" agencies and nonprofits often brings businesses the kind of positive publicity and warm feelings that money can't buy. These uplifting groups include: literacy campaigns, homeless programs, sick or "at-risk" children, the elderly, arts councils, blood drives, food drives, Big Brother and Sister programs, the environment, medical research, AIDS awareness, anti-drunk driving programs, and a host of others.

- J.C. Penney sponsored anti-drug presentations over its local television network by Plays for Living, a Manhattan acting troupe. That was "good for business," according to Jeanette Diegel, Penney's Community Relations Manager. "It shows people we care."

- When Montgomery Ward sponsored a campaign to deter car thefts in Boston, its $1 million investment in public service announcements generated air time worth approximately twenty times that amount in conventional advertising — and also delivered the message that the store cared as much about crime as it did about sales. The PSAs had an "awareness" level of nearly 75% in the fifty-one markets in which they were seen. The city credited the campaign with reducing the city's auto theft rate by 26%.

- Any promotion that nurtures trees is good business. Trees are beautiful, and are also our most efficient anti-pollution devices. They cost little, grow for free, require negligible upkeep, absorb carbon monoxide and carbon dioxide, and give out oxygen. A power company opening a new Connecticut coal-burning plant contributed $2 million to an environmental project for planting fifty-two million trees in Guatemala. The Costa Rican Minister of Natural Resources, in collaboration with American Express Bank and the Nature Conservancy, is exchanging debt for preservation of the rainforest.

- Absolut vodka's Christmas magazine ad featured arctic animals such as penguins and polar bears, and said, "Every animal and plant on this page is in danger of extinction. And every day, you make hundreds of decisions that will affect their fate. To have peace on Earth, we must first make peace with the Earth." The ad offers environmental tips such as replacing paper towels with rags and reusing shopping bags.

- McDonald's polishes its public image with Ronald McDonald Houses, which provide a home away from home for families of seriously ill or injured children.

- SpeeDee Oil Change & Tune-up saves the city of New Orleans $200,000 a year by changing the oil in police cars for free as part of a three-year public service program — and locals remembered the company when it was time to get their oil changed or cars tuned.

- The National Reading Incentive Program, BOOK IT!, motivates children to read with an unbeatable combination: pizza and praise. A student who meets a monthly reading quota can go to the local Pizza Hut, where they'll be personally congratulated by the manager and given a one-topping Personal Pan Pizza. Back at school, the honoree can analyze the pizza's nutritional content with software provided by the National Livestock and Meat Board.

"These aren't community service dollars; these are marketing dollars," said one marketing executive. The trend is so strong that a National

Association of Broadcasters survey showed that more than 75% of television stations involve businesses in their public service campaigns.

BE A COMMUNITY LEADER AND CONTRIBUTOR

If you can be helpful to your community, you will gain friends. People show their gratitude by patronizing your organization.

- Smith & Hawken, a California-based company best known for its popular gardening supply catalog, teamed up with the nonprofit Mill Valley Schools Community Foundation to produce four varieties of holiday wrapping paper using designs by Mill Valley school children. Smith & Hawken paid all the production and promotional costs, and the net profits were turned over to the foundation to finance arts education in Mill Valley schools.

  The company's founder, Paul Hawken, had earlier worked with Doonesbury creator Garry Trudeau to produce "The Great Doonesbury Sellout," a catalog featuring products designed to appeal to Doonesbury devotees, such as a Mr. Butts ashtray and a New World Order Varsity Jacket. All royalties were donated to human rights groups and the homeless, and the project was written up in *INC.* magazine (October, 1991).

- Anita Roddick, founder of The Body Shop and author of *Body and Soul — Profits With Principles* (Crown, 1991), campaigns for environmental causes and encourages employees to volunteer with community groups. Shop windows display posters to protest rainforest burning and the testing of cosmetics on animals. Roddick started a Brazil-nut harvesting project in the Amazonian rainforest and a paper-making facility in Nepal. "Business can have a human face and a social conscience," she says.

- Chevron has found a way to give itself a "socially responsible edge" by sponsoring awards for nonprofit service organizations that turn in outstanding performances despite hard times through strong community support and equally strong management. "This is an opportunity for us to recognize those nonprofits that have shown innovation in extremely trying times," said Skip Rhones, Manager of Corporate Contributions for Chevron. The awards are well publicized and link Chevron with a wide variety of excellent nonprofit organizations.

ENLIGHTENED SELF-INTEREST

The best situation of all is finding a way to contribute to the community that's also in your own best interest.

The March of Dimes, Blue Cross/Blue Shield, NBC affiliate WRC-TV, and others collaborated on a campaign called "Beautiful Babies . . . Right From the Start" that had a significant impact on Washington, D.C.'s high infant mortality rate by encouraging pregnant women to seek prenatal care.

Blue Cross/Blue Shield donated $271,000, and WRC-TV produced news spots, specials, and public service announcements that acknowledged the contribution. The campaign got a phenomenal three hundred fifty gross rating points a week, three or four times more exposure than heavy hitters like Coca-Cola might buy.

The March of Dimes mailed more than sixty thousand pregnant women coupon books worth $700 that could be applied to baby needs ranging from vitamins to clothing to child care classes. To validate the coupons, mothers-to-be had to see doctors for prenatal care at city-approved clinics. After eighteen months, prenatal visits to public health clinics had increased 22% and infant deaths had declined 6%.

"The station gets a vehicle to build viewer loyalty and keep the regulators happy," says Jerry Wishnow, President of the Wishnow Group, a broadcasting consulting firm in Marblehead, Massachusetts, that developed this Walk Your Talk cross-promotion. "The corporate sponsor gets millions of dollars worth of air time." Blue Cross/Blue Shield not only got about $2 billion worth of air time for their $271,000 investment in the "Beautiful Babies" campaign, but saved some $1.5

million in health care costs for low birth weight babies. The nonprofit March of Dimes got their work done and their mission accomplished.

Everyone involved in this campaign — the nonprofit, the city, the corporation, and the media — reaped far more publicity and good will than they could have bought through conventional advertising. And they made an enormous contribution to Washington's newborns and their mothers.

BEWARE OF BACKFIRES

Efforts to appear socially responsible or to promote worthwhile causes can backfire if they aren't genuine and well considered. Check both your own intentions and those of the organization with which you are considering Walk Your Talk cross-promotion, so that you don't run into trouble:

- Air Canada contributed nearly $1 million to a 1982 expedition to climb Mt. Everest at a time when it was also laying off workers, reducing schedules, and suffering financial losses. It hoped that a spectacular ascent would offset the criticisms. When three guides died in the attempt, which was eventually aborted, the airline was linked in the public mind with "disaster" as well as "excess."

- RJR-MacDonald, a tobacco giant, paid $1.7 million to sponsor the Canadian Ski Association for five years — but one champion skier publicly refused to accept their trophy because of the health risks associated with cigarettes. The company later gained even more notoriety when its name was invoked constantly by health groups lobbying the Canadian government to ban such sponsorships, calling them a bad influence on young people.

- Fuji Photo Film paid $6 million to the International Olympic Committee to be named "official film" of the 1984 Olympics — but rival Kodak bought television time on the "official network" (ABC) and sponsored several events, which gave its logo at least as much exposure as Fuji got, for only about $500,000.

CHECKLIST FOR CHOOSING THE RIGHT CAUSE

If you are a business that is considering Walk Your Talk cross-promotion with a worthwhile cause, ask yourself the following questions:

1. What is the market you want to reach, and will Walk Your Talk cross-promoting with this particular organization help you reach it? The connection can be direct or indirect. If you cross-promote with the Sierra Club, you have direct access to its members and other audiences concerned with the environment. Waldenbooks and American Express took a more indirect approach when they supported the adult literacy program. They were probably less interested in reaching Reading Is Fundamental staff and clients than they were in reaching those who heard or read about RIF — a literate market who read and bought books.

2. Is there some connection between your business and the organization's work? It won't do the owner of a music store any harm to work with the hospital thrift shop, but he or she might generate a better Walk Your Talk cross-promotion (and wider networking) with the symphony's thrift shop. Try to focus on a concern that is synergistic with your business. The Home Depot, for instance, supports causes involved with affordable housing.

3. Is this cause known and respected among your potential customers? Does the message it delivers support the message you want to send? If your customers are intimidated, made uncomfortable, or put off by this organization's message, the Walk Your Talk cross-promotion won't do much good — and may actually do you harm. Vegetarians or pet owners, for instance, might be put off by a Big Brother program that teaches boys to hunt.

4. Does this cause matter to your prospective customers? Do they have any personal contact with it? Does it connect with their values and interests, or is it just a nice idea that has little impact on their lives?

5. Is this a good investment in terms of media exposure and/or good will? You may be contributing more money than your partner;

make sure that you actually want to reach their market, and that you'll get a certain level of exposure.

6. Are you using your partner to repair your public image? A better investment of time, energy, and money might be to refrain from further actions that damage your image and reputation.

7. Do you consider your partner an equal, or do you believe that they should do things your way because you're putting up the money? This attitude can come back to haunt you and lead to failed partnerships and unsuccessful, even damaging, Walk Your Talk cross-promotions. What can you do to make the partnership equitable and share power equally?

CHECKLIST FOR CHOOSING THE RIGHT BUSINESS

If you are a nonprofit organization or "do-good" government agency, ask yourself these questions before launching a Walk Your Talk cross-promotion with a business — no matter how much money they're putting into the pot:

1. Will working with this business help you reach the people you want to reach? Make sure that you will touch your audience in some way, and that the benefit to you is more than mere cash.

2. Is this business doing anything that conflicts with your organization's stated goals, interests, and mission? Walk Your Talk cross-promotions with cigarette companies, for instance, have caused trouble for a variety of nonprofits and even other businesses.

3. What opinions will your clients and public form about you, based on your association with this business? Everything you do makes a statement. Organizations that promote health, for instance, must be careful about associations with such products as alcoholic beverages, which can endanger health and safety. Some liquor companies run successful Walk Your Talk cross-promotions to deter drunk driving, but these partnerships must be handled carefully.

4. Does the business have a public relations problem that they want to solve or disguise by their association with you? Consider why the business is seeking you out as a partner. How might that affect your potential clients' opinion of you and their willingness to use your service?

5. How might your association with this business affect other funding opportunities? Fast cash from a mildly unsavory business could have a negative impact on future funding from a more consistent, long-term source.

6. Do you feel like an equal partner in the Walk Your Talk cross-promotion? What are you giving and what are you getting? Do you feel obligated to the business in any inappropriate way? Do you feel like a "poor relation," or do you feel as if your opinions are heard and respected?

Again, consult "The Walk Your Talk Cross-promotion Partners' Bill of Rights" if there is any question about the equality of the partnership.

GETTING STARTED

What can you do to become become part of America's new promotional dream team of socially responsible businesses and worthy nonprofit causes? Here are seven quick start-up ideas. Use them as springboards to Walk Your Talk cross-promotions that you design specifically for your organizations and your community.

1. Create your own local awards for effective management of nonprofit organizations, as Chevron did on a national level. This is an inexpensive, generous way to acknowledge and become associated with nonprofits. In doing the research to discover which organizations deserve the awards, you'll do valuable networking and may find excellent Walk Your Talk cross-promoting partners.

2. Donate half of a day's or an evening's receipts to a nonprofit and make an event of the presentation, perhaps at your place of business.

3. Let a nonprofit use your parking lot, grounds, or building for an event. (Don't forget to check into liability first.)

4. Contact area churches and find out what kinds of outreach programs they have that relate to your business. One clothing store gave customers discounts on new items if they brought in old clothing to donate to a church homeless program.

5. Donating your products or service instead of cash creates more promotional punch. If a local nonprofit is holding an auction and asks you for $100, offer to donate $150 worth of merchandise instead. You spend less, make a larger donation, and get increased exposure for your product.

6. Offer your product to school kids who maintain certain grade averages, or who improve their grades a certain amount.

7. Get involved with "breakfast clubs" that meet to network and share ideas. Invite them to meet at your place of business, and propose projects that involve nonprofits.

Remember, both partners should look for high visibility and low risk. If you do your homework and have a genuine commitment to making the alliance a win-win situation, this can be the best kind of Walk Your Talk cross-promotion for everyone concerned.

SUMMARY

Whether you are a business or a worthy cause, Walk Your Talk cross-promoting can yield unexpected benefits and make you feel good. Both partners can reach people they might never reach otherwise, and expand their marketing and promotional horizons — but you must be careful to ensure that the partnership is co-equal and mutually respectful.

THE WALK YOUR TALK CROSS-PROMOTION PARTNERS' BILL OF RIGHTS

Whether you know your Walk Your Talk cross-promotion partners well, or only slightly, you should agree on some basic standards of conduct beyond your promotion or marketing strategies. These may seem obvious, but discussing and agreeing on specific points makes everything go more quickly and smoothly.

These rights and standards are particularly important when one partner comes to the alliance with a seeming advantage in terms of money, size, or power — as is often the case when businesses cross-promote with nonprofit groups or government agencies. "The Walk Your Talk Cross-promotion Partners' Bill of Rights" ensures that one partner does not use another, and that the groups share equal power in the relationship.

1. The plan is mutually beneficial; no one goes begging or gets bought off. Instead of groveling for donations from large corporations, nonprofits and other organizations should look for plans that let them give as much as they get, so that they don't get stuck in the role of "poor relations" to the corporation's "more powerful rich uncle."
Everyone involved should be clear how the plan benefits both partners, and what each partner is contributing.

2. <u>Partners agree to represent themselves and their intentions honestly.</u> If you ever misrepresent your organization's plans or intentions — accidentally or on purpose — it will be hard to recapture people's interest or trust. Go out of your way to spell out your intentions and motivations for doing the Walk Your Talk cross-promotion, even if you're afraid you may scare off potential partners.

For instance, if you want to cross-promote with day care centers because your organization has gotten a reputation for being hard-nosed and money-grubbing, it's better for the day care people to hear it from you and make up their own minds.

3. <u>Partners disclose any potential weaknesses or problems to one another **before** they agree to work together.</u> If your company is dumping toxic waste into the river, the local Audubon group needs to know that before your joint promotion begins. If your CEO is a slum landlord, the Big Brothers and Sisters program should be informed before they become your Walk Your Talk cross-promotion partner.

Share and solicit information on anything that could go wrong, talk about best-case and worst-case scenarios, and discuss how you and your partners will deal with these problems if they do occur. Then make the choice whether or not to go ahead.

4. <u>A positive attitude makes the work easier and more fun.</u> Being genial, easy to work with, and on the lookout for your partners' positive intentions can make Walk Your Talk cross-promoting a pleasure, rather than something you "have" to do in addition to your "regular job."

In a positive atmosphere of collaboration, the whole becomes greater than the sum of the parts. You get better results, greater rewards, and more personal satisfaction.

8

MAKE EACH EMPLOYEE A SALESPERSON

Your employees can be your most powerful marketing and Walk Your Talk cross-promotional assets. They are your direct link with customers, the intangible human connection that keeps people coming back — or not.

Customers are the most important elements in your business, and mutual markets are the foundation of Walk Your Talk cross-promotions, so you want to do everything you can to keep those people happy. Your staff are the people they see and with whom they talk. To most of your customers, you and your organization are your staff.

When you cross-promote, you and your partner can help one another stay alert to your staffs' needs and morale. You can work together on training and incentive programs that help both staffs become better salespeople and cross-promoters — regardless of their job descriptions.

EVERYONE IS IN SALES

Customers make decisions about you and your organization by watching and interacting with your staff. If your employees like what they are doing and how they are being treated, they can be your best salespeople and double their value to your organization. If they aren't happy with you, the organization, or their jobs, then they won't make your customers happy — and they can do more damage than most people realize.

"There is only one thing that counts in a business: building the self-esteem of your employees," says Robert W. Darvin, founder and CEO of Scandinavian Design, Inc. "Nothing else matters, because what they feel about themselves is what they give to your customers. If an employee comes to work not liking his job, not feeling good about himself, you can be sure that your customers will go away not liking or feeling good about your company."

Your job is to energize this powerful sales force and keep it moving in a positive direction.

- The sixteen-year-old kid who helps out at your small appliance store on Saturdays can be your #1 salesperson and drawing card — if he's warm, enthusiastic, and smiles at every customer as if he or she were the most important person in the world. The same young man can also keep people away if he's surly, unresponsive, or rude.

- The busboy at your new vegetarian restaurant has the same kind of power. If he's unpleasant, scruffy, sullen, or too good for the job he's doing — all of which he can communicate to customers without exchanging one word — he will make diners' experience less pleasant and they will (consciously or unconsciously) be less likely to return. By smiling at them and being efficient and courteous, he can have just as strong a positive impact. They may not even be aware of why they felt so good leaving The Chickpea, but they decide to come back again next Saturday.

These two young gentlemen are not working on commission or making six figures, but they have an enormous influence on whether your organization fails, succeeds a little, or succeeds a lot.

THERE ARE NO NEUTRAL MESSAGES

Everything you and your staff do, say, or communicate nonverbally has either a positive effect or a negative effect on customers' opinion of your product or service. If your employees aren't helping your business, the chances are that they're hurting it.

- If your employees do paperwork, talk to friends on the phone, stare into space, or chat among themselves while customers wait to pay for merchandise or ask questions, the message is a hostile one: "You're a nuisance and we don't want you here. We have no interest in this store, our boss, selling merchandise, or you. We're just marking time until we can leave."

- If they overwhelm customers with attention and information without waiting for responses ("Hi, my name is Debbie can I help you have you heard about our sale items on these racks we have some great new sweaters this would be a nice color for you what size do you take . . ."), people often feel pressured, put off, shut down, and dehumanized — especially if they overhear Debbie make the same speech to the next five people who come into the store, discuss her commissions with co-workers, or gossip about other customers.

  If, on the other hand, your employees look customers in the eye, make themselves available in a friendly, genuinely helpful way, and stay sensitive to how much attention people want, then your customers are likely to have a pleasant human interaction that reinforces their good feelings about your organization.

  The message they receive — consciously or unconsciously — is that you can attract good people and keep them because you treat them well and give them incentives to treat your business as they would their own. Over time, that can have a tremendous effect on sales.

HAPPY EMPLOYEES: YOUR BEST INVESTMENT

Personal recommendations and word-of-mouth are the most powerful forms of promotion and Walk Your Talk cross-promotion. They are completely free, and new people arrive prepared to like your product or service. Happy employees stimulate this particularly effective kind of advertising in two ways:

1. **Customers have more positive personal experiences in your place of business.** When they walk away with smiles on their faces, they are more likely to tell their friends about the pleasant experience they had at your store, or that nice young woman who helped them.

2. **Employees who genuinely like their work create positive attitudes about your organization among their family and friends.** You'd be surprised how much business your staff can generate among their own family and friends if they're smiling when they talk about work.

Creating an enthusiastic staff is one of the best investments you can make in your organization.

ARE YOUR PEOPLE SMILING WHEN THEY LEAVE WORK?

The best test of whether your employees are truly happy and enthusiastic about their jobs and your organization is this: do they promote your organization even when they aren't at work?

The main complaints that people voice about their jobs are:

1. Unfair or unequal treatment

2. Exploitation

3. Arbitrary management decisions

One antidote is to make sure you're not treating people unfairly or unequally, exploiting them, or making arbitrary management decisions. Another is to keep them informed of what is going on in your organization, level with them if there is trouble and explain decisions to them, tell them what they can do to help, and make it worth their while to be positive about their jobs and the organization.

Everyone wants to feel respected and appreciated. If you treat your staff with respect and appreciation, that's how they will treat your customers.

OPENING DOORS

In some ways, your employees are your most important customers. Approach them as you would your customers: find out what *they* want, rather than telling them what you think they should get.

These are some factors that influence how people feel about their jobs:

1. Do they they feel appreciated and respected?

2. Do they enjoy their tasks?

3. Do they like and respect you?

4. Do they have a positive opinion of your product or service?

5. Do they feel they are paid what they deserve?

You are the best judge of whether to gather this information informally, or to sit down with each employee and let them know that you are interested in how they feel about their jobs.

Some staff members may be nervous or uncomfortable in an interview situation. Try to break the ice and put them at ease. Ask them about their future plans, and listen to what they tell you about themselves and your organization. Don't try to fill every gap in the conversation; silence prompts them to talk. If there is a problem, give them feedback in a constructive way that encourages them to do better.

Begin establishing personal relationships with your employees, so that it's easier for them to talk openly and frankly with you, and easier for you to communicate with them.

Open a regular channel of communication — weekly staff meetings, informal conversations, scheduled lunches with individuals or departments — so that you have a comfortable and nonthreatening way to keep current with them. People feel important and recognized when they have a regular forum in which to be heard, and finding out about problems early helps you solve them more quickly and easily.

WHAT YOU CAN LEARN FROM EMPLOYEES

Another way to make employees feel respected and appreciated is to ask their opinion on issues that affect your organization. As the bridge between you and your customers, they are in a unique position to give you invaluable answers to these kinds of questions:

1. What should we do to improve our product or service?

2. How can we implement those improvements?

3. What else can we do with this product?

4. What other ways can we market it?

5. What similar products can we make with minimal additional investment?

6. What kinds of feedback are we getting from our sales force and our customers?

Let your employees help you gather information about your customers as well. Train them how to put customers at ease and make them feel welcome, and also how to find out more about them. There are friendly, subtle ways for your staff to ask customers these kinds of questions:

- Where do you live?

- Where do you work?

- What do you do for entertainment, and where?

- Do you have any children?

- Have you seen or heard about products and services better than ours?

- What would you improve about our product or service?

HELP YOUR EMPLOYEES WIN

Whether you are involved in a Walk Your Talk cross-promotion or doing business as usual, give your employees the tools they need to do a good job and win. Use these three guidelines:

1. TRAIN THEM THOROUGHLY to do anything they are expected to do: specific tasks, talking to customers, sales, etc. Give them all the information and tools they need to do a good job. Make sure they understand your organization's philosophy, point of view, and internal structure, as well as your product or service.

2. TREAT THEM WITH FAIRNESS AND RESPECT. This is a question of attitude. Think of your staff as the players on a team, and yourself as the captain. Some specific ways you can show fairness and respect are:

- Don't play favorites.

- Express your appreciation in tangible and intangible ways. Give them verbal pats on the back, as well as bonuses and incentives.

- Show a genuine personal interest in them.

- Establish clear lines of communication, so that they know who is their boss and to whom they should take problems.

- Let them know what kinds of raises they can expect, at what intervals, and how the level of their performance will affect the amount of the raise.

3. MAKE THEM PLAYERS: GIVE THEM A STAKE IN THE ORGANIZATION. There are three main ways to give your employees an emotional and financial stake in your organization:

Let them participate in making decisions

Find out what is important to them, and give them as much of it as you can. Ask for their input on both substantive issues and the more mechanical aspects of their work: hours, uniforms, tasks, procedures, etc.

Some factors can be adjusted and some cannot, but employees will at least know that their opinions have been registered. Tell them that you're willing to work toward changes, and be flexible when you can. Adjusting rules or work hours might pay off, even if they are uncomfortable for you at first. Happy employees generate more sales, give better service, make your place of business more pleasant to be in — and all those things enhance profits.

When your employees help make decisions, they have an investment in your organization and its success. The organization's best interests coincide more closely with their own.

Give incentives and bonuses

When people know that they will be compensated for their contribution to the organization's profits, they often respond by working harder and doing a better job.

Benefits, incentives, and bonuses all have different purposes.

Benefits: Benefits are available to all employees; they are special features that attract people to work for your organization. In addition to insurance and other standard employment benefits, give your staff deep discounts on your merchandise. For instance, salespeople in a clothing store shouldn't stand around looking great in competitors' suits or dresses. Workers in computer stores should have computers at their disposal. Customers can tell the difference between a prepared pitch and personal experience.

Incentives: Incentives reward and recognize outstanding work, good will, or improvement. Find incentives that encourage employees to go out of their way for the business, to provide fast and friendly service, and to work as a team.

Choose incentives that relate to *their* needs and values, not necessarily to yours. Make the prize a gift certificate at a record store, for instance, not your three favorite Frank Sinatra albums.

When you cross-promote, you and your partner can exchange staff benefits and incentives. A hair salon, clothing store, bath boutique, or body care store might offer one another's staffs their products or services as incentives.

Here are some ways you can use incentives:

- Give each employee fifty special cards entitling the bearers to discounts. Have your staff sign each one and distribute them to their family, friends, acquaintances, and even people they meet on the street. Your employees feel good about giving people something of value, and you get new customers. Make it a contest and give an incentive to the employee whose signature appears on the most cards that are returned. (You can run a similar contest with your regular customers.)

- Pam Reynolds, President of Phoenix Textiles, invented a new currency called "bird bills" as an incentive. Staff could earn the play money for excellent performance in ten clearly defined areas. To foster teamwork, they could transfer bills to other employees' accounts if someone helped them. At the end of a year, Phoenix hosted a cocktail party and auction at which staff used their "bird bills" to buy items such as movie tickets, a cruise, a fax machine, and sleeping bags. The total cost of the incentive program was about $15,000, including the dinner and the auction. That may seem high, but the program's cost per person was only about $214 and Reynolds believes she got a good return on her investment.

Bonuses: Bonuses relate strictly to the employee's contribution to your bottom line and reflect his or her direct contribution to your earnings. These rewards shouldn't be restricted to salespeople.

A supermarket manager received a letter from one of his regular customers, an elderly woman whom he knew because she lived in the neighborhood. She wrote that over the past year she had been hurried and treated rudely several times, and was considering taking her business elsewhere until last Tuesday, when a busy but courteous worker went out of his way to carry her shopping bags to the car. The young man was given a $50 bonus and a letter of appreciation, both of which made him feel great and work even harder.

Many companies give bonuses for "upselling" another product with the first one — a Coke with the fries, an oil change with the tire rotation, pet foods and accessories with the pets — especially in difficult economic times.

Honor your employees publicly

It's nice to be honored among your co-workers, but it means even more if your boss or manager wants to tell the world about you. Three ways to honor employees publicly are:

- Select an "Employee of the Month" and place displays with his or her picture in your store. Tie the honor to performance. Remember that the recipient is more likely to respond with pride and enthusiasm if you don't just rotate the award among all your workers. If you also use the "Employee of the Month" in newspapers and other advertising, be sure to mention the good work or public service that this person has performed (e.g., blood donations, volunteer work, etc.) and always note how long he or she has worked for you.

- Use employees in your advertising. For years, ads for the San Francisco-based apparel company Esprit featured their own staff in Esprit clothing, which was theirs to keep.

- Let the local media and business publications know about your employees' accomplishments: sales records, promotions, etc. This not only acknowledges your staff, but generates free advertising.

SEVEN WAYS TO HELP YOUR STAFFS CROSS-PROMOTE

Your employees can energize a Walk Your Talk cross-promotion more effectively than any sign, handout, mailing, or event by giving glowing reports to customers about the other organization.

Take active steps to ensure that your employees feel as enthusiastic about your partner's organization as they do about yours. Here are seven things you can to do generate that kind of positive and proactive promotion:

1. Make sure they know that your Walk Your Talk cross-promotion is based on mutual markets, and that your customers should be the focus of everything they do. Let them know how important it is to go out of their way to make customers happy.

2. Invite your Walk Your Talk cross-promotion partner to speak to your staff at a special meeting so that they know everything they need to know about the other organization and feel good about your partner. Make sure they understand that they are important, respected members of the Walk Your Talk cross-promotion team, and that both of you depend on them to communicate your message to customers.

Have your partner bring along a small gift, sample, or coupon so that your people can try the other product or service. This gives them a sense of its value, and makes them feel included and appreciated.

Then you do the same with your partner's staff.

3. Create Walk Your Talk cross-promotional incentives. Find a way for your employees to benefit from the Walk Your Talk cross-promotion.

- Laser Vision Centers, a provider of laser equipment and medical marketing services in St. Louis, has independent sales representatives for related products mention Laser Vision's name to their physician clients and get the doctors to block out time to meet with a Laser Vision salesperson. If the Laser Vision presentation leads to a sale, the contact gets a finder's fee of 10% of Laser Vision's fee. That's less than what a full-time Laser Vision rep would receive, but enough to make it worth the effort.

   "These people are in the neighborhood and know the people we want to sell to," says Jack Klobnak, CEO of Laser Vision. He estimates that this strategy generates 20-25% of Laser Vision's leads. "If we get the opportunity to make the pitch, we make the sale about 40% of the time."

- As part of a video store's Walk Your Talk cross-promotion with a convenience store, employees mentioned the other business when people checked out at the register. They handed each customer "Bob sent me" or "Karen sent me" discount cards to present at the other business, and earned free video rentals and coupons good for $3 at the convenience store based on how many of their customer cards were returned.

4. Schedule a time for your staffs to meet one another. If Sally and Rick at the convenience store know Bob and Karen at the video store, everyone will put more energy into the Walk Your Talk cross-promotion. Customers will sense the difference if Bob actually knows Rick when he says, "Tell Rick I sent you over." Let a natural synergy emerge between the two staffs. Consider a joint staff party before, during, or after the Walk Your Talk cross-promotion.

5. Create joint outreach and/or sales training programs for both groups of employees that enhance their sales skills, improve customer relations, and teach them specific techniques for promoting the other group.

6. Rely on employees to give you information about how the Walk Your Talk cross-promotion is going. They are your best source of information, and asking for their input and opinion is another way to let them know how important they are to you. Ask your employees:

- How are customers responding to the Walk Your Talk cross-promotion?

- What are people saying about it when they come to your place of business?

- How is it working out for the employees themselves?

- What problems have they encountered?

- What can be done to solve these problems?

- How can the Walk Your Talk cross-promotion be improved?

7. Acknowledge their efforts. Include your staffs in some aspects of your debriefing. Tell them what the results were and thank them for their specific contributions. Find out what worked for them, and what didn't. Ask what you can do next time to make a promotion work better. Be sure they know how much you appreciate their feedback and their good work throughout the Walk Your Talk cross-promotion.

SUMMARY

Treating employees with respect and appreciation, and letting them participate in decision-making whenever possible, makes them more enthusiastic about your organization. They become premier salespeople, regardless of their positions.

CHAPTER 9

MAKE NEWS: HOW TO ACCESS THE LOCAL MEDIA

When you or your partner do something unusual, exciting, or particularly valuable, you become eligible for free publicity that would otherwise cost hundreds, perhaps hundreds of thousands, of dollars. It's called media coverage, and it's not difficult to get — if you know how to play the game.

When you cross-promote, you double your chances to cash in on this free form of advertising.

When socially responsible businesses cross-promote with worthwhile nonprofit causes, the opportunities multiply exponentially.

MAKING NEWS IS MAKING MONEY

Coverage by the news media is the best form of advertising because:

- **It is free**.

- **It is credible**.

Many public relations professionals believe that any media coverage is good. They agree with P.T. Barnum, who said, "I don't care what you say about me; just spell my name right." Media coverage can be fun, but simply reading your name in the paper or seeing yourself on television isn't enough to promote your organization — and that should be your main goal.

Give careful thought to exactly what you want to say, and how and to whom you want to say it, before you open your doors to throngs of reporters or tell the papers to stop the presses. "The power of the press" is no joke; make sure that power is working *for* you, not *against* you.

Remember: You have to *make* news in order to make the news. Don't rely on the media to create your success; rather, create your own success and give the media a break by allowing them to cover it. Then let that coverage take you to new heights.

News that is genuine, interesting, and informative is the media's bread and butter. It's how they live. If you have it or can generate it, then you have what they want and need. They'll be more than happy to give you free publicity in exchange.

WHICH MEDIA IS BEST?

Media coverage can mean anything from a small mention in a local news story to being featured on CBS's "Sixty Minutes." Your detailed market research pays off again here. You know exactly where your customers and potential customers get their information, so you save money by targeting exactly the right media.

Some of the most useful media are:

Newspapers. Consider each section of the paper — news, business, style, sports, etc. — as a separate publication and write directly to the editor of that section by name, not by job title. Address your letter or news release to John Smith, not the generic "Sports Editor." If you don't know the name of the person who edits the section where you want your item to appear, call the paper and find out.

There are several ways to approach newspapers:

• Press releases. This is a short, one- to two-page statement of your information, written in the form of a news story. It contains all the specifics you want people to know: names, descriptions and purpose of event or announcement, dates, times, and places. These are the traditional Who, What, When, Where, and Why. Press releases have a conventional format that is outlined in most publicity and public relations manuals. A particularly good description appears in *Marketing Without Advertising* (Nolo Press, 1989) by Michael Phillips and Salli Rasberry. Follow up your press release with a phone call to the person to whom you sent it. Be clear, brief, helpful, and businesslike.

• Feature stories. These are generally longer than newspaper stories, and they must entertain or enlighten as well as inform. What is the "hook" or angle that makes your story irresistible **to the publication's audience?**

Also consider writing "service features" for your local paper. If you do the paper's work for them — giving them a ready-made story that readers will find interesting or valuable — they are likely to print these articles. Successful feature stories are *factual*, *brief*, and *modest*. If you don't feel you can write them yourself, hire a ghostwriter for a small fee.

Daily newspapers add pages during the holidays to accommodate the extra advertising, and then fill the "news holes" with syndicated stories, but editors may prefer contributions from a local source —

you. A dry cleaner might write a feature on "Professional Secrets for Removing the Ten Most Common Spots and Stains." A dentist could write "The Power of a Healthy Smile" or "Protecting Your Teeth From Holiday Excesses."

You don't have to mention your organization by name in the story; simply give yourself a byline ("by Joan Silver, Owner, Joan's Antiques" or "by Steven Parker, D.D.S.").

You and your Walk Your Talk cross-promoting partners can co-author these features, and may even turn them into regular columns. The local gym or workout center might team up with a sports physician to create "Staying Healthy While You Stay in Shape." A market and gourmet cookware store might co-author a recipe column.

- Contacting Individual Reporters. If you've noticed that one reporter is usually assigned stories about your field, call him or her and introduce yourself. Volunteer to be a resource on the subject, and establish a personal connection. Find a "hook" that makes your own story interesting to the public, and suggest that the reporter do a piece on your organization.

- Letters to the Editor. People often forget this section when casting about for publicity ideas, but it has a high readership and — unlike news and feature stories — lets you say whatever you want, however you want to say it.

Magazines. These include local magazines, trade magazines, small business publications, neighborhood newsletters, and the local Sunday supplements. Contact them as you would newspapers, or write a query letter outlining your story and follow up with a phone call.

Radio and Television. Radio and television have a daily need for news, features, editorials, public service announcements, guests on talk shows, and call-ins. Don't forget your local cable stations. Contact the directors of the news, editorial, and public service departments or the producers of individual shows (by name) with your press release, and follow up with a phone call.

For television, don't forget to include a picture or video tape, and tell them about your other visual materials: charts, pictures, etc.

If you and your partner have information to share on an ongoing basis (attorneys, physicians, tax consultants, fashion experts, psychologists, etc.), you may even create your own daily or weekly program — or appear as regular guests on a local show.

Neighborhood papers. Your chances of being featured in — or writing features for — these papers are excellent. If yours is a neighborhood business, you also target your audience very effectively.

Weekly "shopper" or "advertisers." Many of these feature stories on local organizations as well.

Create your own newsletter for your customers with tips, funny stories, neighborhood news, and discount coupons.

Fillers: Prepare one- or two-paragraph items about your organization or field that newspapers, magazines, neighborhood papers, or "advertisers" can use to fill gaps at the bottom of news columns. Attach a note explaining that you are submitting them as fillers to be used as needed.

The possibilities for media coverage are limited only by your imagination. The best medium for you is the one that reaches the most potential customers, most often, in the most powerful way.

YOUR MEDIA MAILING LIST

The people on your media mailing list will receive your press releases and announcements. To create a media mailing list tailored especially for your organization, gather the names, addresses, phone numbers, and office hours of news, editorial, and public service directors at area television and radio stations; producers of shows that might feature your organization; reporters who cover your field; editors of sections of the local paper where your stories are likely to appear; and editors of smaller papers, magazines, and other publications.

To create a media mailing list for your Walk Your Talk cross-promotion, merge your list with your partner's.

As you start to network and make other media contacts, add these to your mailing list. Also add opinion leaders and freelance writers who may see a way to convert a news release into a magazine article.

MATCH THE MEDIA TO YOUR MESSAGE — AND TO YOUR AUDIENCE

Target the media that your customers find most credible, and that reaches them most often in the most effective ways.

"It's not just the number of eyeballs you reach, but also the environment you reach them in," says Michael J. Hedge, Senior Vice President and Director of Media Services for BBDO advertising agency in Chicago. The agency represents chewing gum giant William Wrigley, Jr., and considers cable television the key to reaching that company's crucial twelve- to twenty-four-year-old market.

Since you are reaching out to new people with your Walk Your Talk cross-promotion, you may find yourself involved with media that are unfamiliar to you. When a video store in Marin County, California, linked up with the Registrar of Voters on a voter registration Walk Your Talk cross-promotion, the video store found itself on the news pages and voter registration found itself in the entertainment section. Both groups reached people who might not have otherwise known about them.

The two keys to using media effectively are:

1. Know where your customers go for news, entertainment, and information. Why waste time, energy, and perhaps money on getting media coverage that doesn't reach your customers? You wouldn't buy advertising for skateboards in a magazine for retirees, or promote at-home medical supplies in a teen magazine.

Mentally follow your typical customer through a normal day. Observe the different media with which he or she comes into contact: the radio while driving to work; a newspaper; professional journals in the mail at work; magazines at the dentist's office; television at home.

Which media do your customers see or hear most often? Which affects them most powerfully? You will answer these questions in more detail when you develop your joint media plan.

2. **Learn how to work with your targeted media.** Just as newspapers have business, sports, politics, entertainment, local, and "style" sections — and many have "zoned editions" for different areas or neighborhoods — every medium is divided into many smaller segments that serve their own unique audiences and have their own schedules and deadlines.

You need to understand and accommodate the specific needs and deadlines of the segments that reach your customers best. What time do they need information to make their next edition? How much lead time do they need for what kinds of stories? If you don't know, call them up and ask.

DESIGN A JOINT MEDIA PLAN

You and your Walk Your Talk cross-promoting partners identified the potential customers you share when you did your marketing plan in Chapter 6. Now it's just a question of finding out where that joint audience gets its news, information, and entertainment — and targeting those segments of the media.

To pinpoint the best media for your Walk Your Talk cross-promotion, you need answers to the following questions:

1. What newspapers do your potential customers read?

2. What magazines do they subscribe to or buy? For news? For entertainment?

3. What television shows do they watch?

4. Do they listen to radio? When?

5. What kind of music do they buy? When? Where?

6. What professional journals do they read?

7. Where do they get their news?

8. What do they do for entertainment: movies, theater, concerts, restaurants? What kinds of movies, theater, concerts, restaurants?

9. Where and when do they get their information about the part of their lives affected by your product or service?

The best way to gather this information is to ask your customers. As always, make it worth their while. Offer a gift or discount to people who take the time to fill out your questionnaire. Make it easy for them to complete by letting them sit down and fill it out at your place of business, or take it home and mail it in.

When you've gathered this information, make a list of the ten most effective media to target. Design ways to attract and hold the attention of those media using the suggestions in the rest of this chapter.

HOW TO GET AND KEEP MEDIA ATTENTION

There are two basic ways to get and keep the media's attention:

1. **MAKE GENUINE NEWS.** This is the fuel on which the media run. If you do something that is truly newsworthy, they will want to cover it. The people who decide what will be printed or broadcast strive to serve the interests of their readers, listeners, and viewers. They also want to attract more readers, listeners, and viewers than anybody else, so the material they use has to be more interesting,

fresher, and more valuable to their "customers" than what their competitors print or air.

The question they ask themselves, silently and aloud in editorial conferences, is: *"What about this story is of special interest to our audience?"* If they don't come up with a good, solid answer, they don't use the story.

To get your stories used, and to become known as a reliable news source, learn how to play news editor. Before you send out a press release, put on your news editor hat and ask yourself *what is unique, special, and compelling about your story to that particular medium's audience?* If you don't come up with an answer that is both exciting and credible, work on the story until you do.

Make sure you're really making news — creating events, generating information, doing the unusual — and not just going through the motions of sending out press releases.

2. BECOME A SOURCE OF INFORMATION ABOUT YOUR FIELD. In return for ongoing background information, they may quote you and use your organization's name. You'll be particularly valuable to them if you keep abreast of the news, so that you can comment when world events impact your industry.

THE FOUR BIG QUESTIONS

To check whether or not your story is newsworthy, ask yourself four important questions:

1. IS WHAT YOU ARE DOING TIMELY? Is it important *right now*? Does it relate to some current event, national crisis, or public concern? Does it refer to a person who is currently in the news, or to an issue that affects that person?

A toy store might offer information on educational toys after reports of poor academic test results in public schools. Health organizations might offer information in the wake of announcements about certain conditions (heart disease, cancer, etc.) or about people in the news with these illnesses.

2. ARE OTHERS TELLING A SIMILAR STORY? IF SO, WHAT MAKES YOUR MESSAGE UNIQUE? You need to distinguish your story from all the others, and make it one-of-a-kind. Your unique "hook" may be an unusual Walk Your Talk cross-promoting partnership.

Connecticut's Fairfield University teamed up with the Food Bank of Fairfield County for a project that gave computer students practical experience designing programs to help the nonprofit keep track of food arriving from various sources for soup kitchens. The team was unusual enough to be written up in *Business Week* and other publications, and worked so well that the students have moved on to tackle similar projects involving shelters for the homeless and other community service programs.

3. WHAT IS THE DISTINCTLY LOCAL ANGLE TO YOUR STORY? Find something that makes your message especially interesting or intriguing to people in your own community.

- The local paper may not be interested in yet another article about the United Way, but it might jump on the story of one little boy in your community whose life was turned around by a United Way agency. If you are the local United Way, make sure they find out about him.

- The Red Cross may do wonderful work for hurricane victims two thousand miles away, but your papers may be more interested in the story of one volunteer from your town working around the clock in a faraway state.

- A plant nursery owner gave away pine tree seedlings with each $20 purchase. It was a commendable gesture, but nobody knew about it until she called up a local Girl Scout troop and suggested that they make a project of acquiring twenty trees and planting them in a community park. The nursery owner sold $400 in goods, both she and the Scouts got wide, glowing press coverage, the town got twenty new pine trees, and everybody felt great.

4. WHAT VISUAL ELEMENTS MAKE YOUR STORY COME ALIVE? IN EVERY MEDIUM, THE REPORTER WILL SAY, "DON'T TELL ME; SHOW ME." If your story can be photographed or easily illustrated, you have a better chance of getting coverage. Television is a particularly visual medium; your story must be seen as well as heard. On radio, the power comes from supplying a distinctive "sound bite" that seizes listeners' attention.

Always put yourself in the reporter or editor's shoes, and determine what will "sell" your story before you approach each medium.

THE SEVEN SECRETS TO GETTING SUCCESSFUL COVERAGE

Here are the seven secrets to getting great coverage by the media:

1. BE ON TIME, AND BE BRIEF. There are five ways to use time to your advantage:

A. Give reporters enough notice to cover your story.

B. Call only if your news is current.

C. If possible, release information the day after a holiday, when news may be scarce.

D. Anticipate events in your field before they break, and call a reporter with a scoop.

E. Respond immediately when news breaks in your industry. You can't call a reporter and say, "Remember that event last month . . ."

Being brief is especially important for radio and television. You must sum up your key points in a few short sentences. You can offer reporters a longer, off-the-record "backgrounder" if they are completely unfamiliar with the event, but the best response to any question is usually the shortest.

2. BE SOCIALLY RESPONSIBLE. Teaming up with worthy nonprofits, or simply doing good works on your own, are increasingly effective ways to generate press coverage. People like to read and see "good news," and the media like to run stories that make their audiences feel good.

- This story was syndicated by *USA Today* in August 1991: "Great news for the socially conscious. Now you can display environmentally correct behavior at the breakfast table. Two new cereals — Rainforest Crisp and Rainforest Granola — are arriving in stores now, the first offerings from Rainforest Products, backed by such global-minded celebrities as Bobbie Weir of the Grateful Dead, guru Ram Dass and Ben Cohen of Ben and Jerry's Ice Cream fame.

  "'It's a 100% everybody wins situation,' says Weir. He'll donate all income from his investment to rain-forest protection programs and Cultural Survival, a group that helps people in affected regions earn money by using the fruits of the forest instead of cutting down trees. Rainforest Products will donate at least 7% of profits to environmental groups and pay 5% over market price for nuts."

- Walk Your Talk cross-promoting with MADD (Mothers Against Drunk Driving) and the public school system was a bonanza for Razcal Corporation of Wayland, Massachusetts, which makes and sells a raspberry-lime soda for the teen market. It was a classic combination of business, nonprofit, and government in which everybody won.

  MADD had tried for years to interest schools in a poster contest with an anti-drinking theme, but few schools responded. Razcal offered to fund and produce a slick direct-mail campaign for the poster contest, which went to four thousand high schools in New England. Three thousand students representing five hundred schools participated. Razcal provided prizes, as well as music and soda for sock hops honoring the winners.

  The total cost of the campaign to Razcal — which also included T-shirts, sweatshirts, hats, drinking cups, raffles, and giving away about one hundred thousand cans of soda — was

$25,000. The promotion got wide coverage in the press and schools, and supermarkets provided point-of-purchase displays to ally themselves with the MADD-Razcal anti-drinking message. Razcal doubled sales between 1989 and 1990 from two hundred fifty thousand cases to five hundred thousand cases.

3. DON'T BRAG. Nobody wants to cover you if you sound like a press release. If you are interviewed for television or radio, avoid mentioning your organization by name; they will introduce you and give your affiliation. Here's an example that combines not bragging with being brief:

> **Question:** When will we see this new technology in the marketplace?

> **Wrong Answer:** I'm glad you asked me that. We here at Widgetech have studied this problem for a long time and we've developed a number of what our founder used to call 'solutions in search of a problem.' As to the one you asked about, it could come as early as the third quarter.

> **Right Answer:** Next October.

4. DON'T MAKE A PEST OF YOURSELF. When you follow up your press release with a phone call, be brief and to the point. Talk about why your event or information would interest readers or viewers — and speak to the reporter's needs, rather than to your own.

Call only when you have something they can't refuse. If you call every month asking if you can be helpful or begging reporters to cover your organization, they move your phone number to the "circular file" and stop taking your calls. Again, put yourself in the reporter or editor's shoes. If you cry "Wolf!" when you don't really have a story, they won't listen when you have something important to say.

5. LOOK FOR UNUSUAL MEDIA, AND STAR IN THEM. Everyone competes for such common media as newspapers, radio, and television. You're more likely to get coverage, and to become a star, in an unusual medium — even if you have to create that medium yourself. Look for new horizons. Some unusual media you might consider are:

- Refrigerator magnets

- Gift boxes or wrapping paper

- A booth at the county fair

- Local late-night television or cable shows

One restaurant owner who was new to town found an unusual, but highly effective, use for his small marketing budget. He delivered a gift certificate for one free meal to every hair stylist in the community — people who spent the whole day talking (and occasionally gossiping) with other people. Word of the restaurant spread faster than wildfire, and he showed a profit his first year.

6. BE AN EXPERT. Don't forget that you are an expert in your field. You deal with something every day that may be a complete mystery to others. Share your wealth of information, and get free publicity in the bargain — or team up with Walk Your Talk cross-promoting partners and become the "double experts" that no media can resist.

- A kitchenware shop owner appeared on local television preparing one of her "Five Gourmet Meals You Can Make in 30 Minutes."

- A toy store owner and an educator speak on "Toys That Help Children To Learn."

- A dress designer and a dry cleaner team up for a presentation on "How To Look Impeccable Without Effort."

If you can land a weekly slot on a local news or talk show, you automatically become a local expert on your field.

- The garden shop owner who appears each Friday on the noon news with tips for producing healthy flowers and vegetables becomes a local celebrity — "the plant lady" — and people are more likely to come to her shop than to her competitors'.

- The hardware store owner who convinces the local cable station to give him a weekly home improvement show becomes "the guy on TV" and can now draw crowds by using a photo in his ads.

7. BE A CELEBRITY. The difference between an expert and a celebrity is only a matter of degree. The "Five Gourmet Meals" speaker started by appearing free at civic and professional lunches. Six months later, she commanded a $200 fee and now speaks all around the country, writes a syndicated column, hosts a call-in radio show, and makes more money from professional appearances than she does from her kitchenware shop.

With some experience, you may find yourself in as much demand as she was. You may not want to launch a career as a public speaker, but you should seriously consider becoming well known for what you do. Even minor celebrity status can make you the person whom reporters call for expert quotes and opinions.

The eighth, unwritten, secret of getting good media coverage is to cross-promote with media. Publicity takes care of itself when you team up with a local newspaper, radio, or television station. Your promotion is their promotion. They are particularly interested in working with worthy causes, so use this to your advantage if you are a cause. If you are a business, remember that you'll get better coverage if you are teamed with an uplifting nonprofit cause.

The more you work with the media, the more contacts you'll develop and the more effective you'll become. Don't be afraid to jump in and begin using this invaluable resource. Look for unique ways that you and your Walk Your Talk cross-promoting partners can work with the press to make what they report more interesting and your organizations more successful.

SUMMARY

The media are an unbeatable source of free publicity, but you must know how to use them. Target your potential customers carefully, match your medium to your audience, and remember that you have to give the media something that's valuable to them — news, information, or entertainment — in return for the free advertising they give you.

The seven secrets to getting great coverage by the media are:

1. Be on time, and be brief.

2. Be socially responsible.

3. Don't brag.

4. Don't make a pest of yourself.

5. Look for unusual media, and star in them.

6. Be an expert.

7. Be a celebrity.

10

ADD SPARKLE: WORKING WITH CELEBRITIES

Your celebrity doesn't have to be the President of the United States or Hollywood's #1 box office attraction. Local, everyday heroes can be just as powerful promoters and cross-promoters as these more famous individuals. Local heroes' good deeds might go unsung if you didn't pull them into the spotlight, and you're giving them a chance to contribute to the community as well.

How do you find local celebrities, and what should you do with them once you have them? Why should they help you out and what trade-off can you make with them?

WHY SHOULD CELEBRITIES WORK WITH YOU?

When you team up with a celebrity, he or she becomes your Walk Your Talk cross-promoting partner. As in every partnership, it's wise to stay aware of what everyone is giving and getting so that no one feels used or resentful.

As Walk Your Talk cross-promoting partners, you and the celebrity want to reach the same audience. Your reasons for reaching that audience may differ slightly, but you are offering celebrities greater visibility for themselves — or their charitable and socially responsible causes — with your particular market.

Many celebrities want to promote worthwhile causes, either because they have a special interest in the cause's work, because they believe it is part of their jobs, or because they consider it a gesture of general good will and a payback for their good fortune. If you can align your Walk Your Talk cross-promotion with that cause — health awareness, disease prevention, vegetarianism, the environment, human or animal rights — they have a reason to work with you.

If you and your partners benefit as well, that's fine with them. After all, you put the Walk Your Talk cross-promotion together and are calling attention to something that's important to them.

"Now that [Marla Maples] is a personality, she wants to direct some of that positive energy toward a good cause," spokesman Chuck Jones told the *New York Post* about the actress' charitable activities, which included making a cash donation to Ted Turner's Better World Society and hosting a fundraiser with Donald Trump for ChildKind, which benefits children with AIDS.

Top athletes who might not stand around your sports store shaking hands with customers all afternoon so that you could sell more tennis shoes may feel honored to do so if a percentage of the proceeds are donated to muscular dystrophy research ... or if the promotion is part of a larger campaign to fight cerebral palsy ... or if you are spearheading a fundraising drive for your local Special Olympics.

Politicians will often step into the limelight, but only if you place them next to something positive for the inevitable newspaper photo or evening news shot — community social programs, literacy awards, homeless shelters, high school sports or academic achievement honorees. If you team up with the Heart Association, the Eagle Scouts, or the Big Brothers and Sisters program, they will be delighted to stand outside your fast food outlet with their arms around an irresistible youngster or a paragon of American youth — but they don't want grandmothers and church groups to see them on the evening news hawking drinks outside of your bar.

A word of caution: Celebrities can carry troublesome baggage, and it's a good idea to check around before you invite them to promote with you. You don't want your shop's walls covered with pictures of the athlete who is charged the next week with drugs or gambling. Nor do you want the politician who's at the bottom of a financial or sexual scandal smiling and waving outside your store.

All celebrities have different interests and goals. Be alert to their individual needs and "rates of exchange," as well as to your own. Make sure they feel they've gotten as much as they gave, and that you've generated good will with them so that they'll work with you again.

WHERE TO FIND CELEBRITIES

Local heroes and celebrities are everywhere in your community, and many of them speak to your potential customers more clearly and effectively than national figures. Your customers can actually meet these people — touch them, shake their hands, talk to them, establish a connection, and create a camaraderie they might not feel with world-famous film actors or sports giants.

Here are some places to find local celebrities:

Local athletes. Athletes have a special tradition of promoting good causes and making themselves available to the public. Most professional athletes find some way to contribute to their communities and/or promote products, and amateurs are often eager to emulate the pros in this way.

People love to meet athletes in the flesh, and sports figures can create a tremendous draw to your place of business. Most kids get a thrill out of meeting even high school, university, or semi-pro players — and it doesn't have to be the quarterback who threw the winning pass, the right fielder who hit the home run, or the guard who scored the winning basket. Put any ten-year-old next to a 6'7" college basketball player, even if he's 24th on a squad of 25, and the little guy's eyes will light up. The same thing can happen to teenage girls.

Don't forget the men and women who won the city golf and tennis tournaments, or the local foot or bike races. Are there any great fishermen or swimmers in your area? A top marathoner? What about oldest and youngest competitor in local sports events? Handicapped athletes? Are there any stories of great courage, of overcoming injuries or adversity to compete?

All of these people are local sports heroes.

Local actors. You'll be amazed how many amateur actors there are in your community, and how eager they are to appear in public even without being paid. Check with your local or area theaters, or look up "Theatrical Agents" in the *Yellow Pages* to find out who these people are. Your customers may have seen them in a play or commercial, and would be delighted to meet them in person. The actors may even be willing to stage a short performance in your place of business.

People who are well known in their field. These include the president of the local or state bar association, the head of the medical society, the local college president or dean of admissions, the athletic coaches, and anyone who has achieved distinction in his or her field.

Watch the newspapers for "hidden celebrities," people who are famous in their own area of endeavor but whose expertise may be virtually unknown to most people: the heads of state or area needlepoint, backgammon, gardening, equestrian, yachting, literary, or artistic groups.

Don't forget about long-time volunteers with medical, child abuse, psychiatric, or blood donation facilities who have been publicly recognized for their contributions.

Government leaders. Politicians rarely turn down a chance to cross-promote if they'll appear to be doing good — and they have excellent connections with the media that virtually ensure press coverage. Government leaders include the mayor, members of Congress, state legislators, local aldermen or supervisors, the head librarian, school board officials — everyone from your U.S. senators down to the dog catcher.

Civic leaders. These people are also quite available — and they have an interest and investment in the community. If you can convince them that Walk Your Talk cross-promoting with you is in the civic interest, or their own personal interest, they will be gracious and compelling additions to your event or promotion. They know how to charm and talk to people, and usually have something to say.

Civic leaders include large donors to local causes (charitable, artistic, civic); bank foundation members; Chamber of Commerce president; ballet, opera or symphony boards; hospital auxiliary board members — anyone who makes a significant contribution to your city's social, political, cultural, or economic life.

Citizen heroes. These people are usually new to celebrity status, and are often glad to help. They are brave firefighters or police officers, the woman who found and returned a wallet containing a large sum of money, the boy who pulled his little brother out of the icy pond.

Watch the papers to find these people. When you see a story that fits with one of your promotional themes, don't be shy about contacting the citizen heroes. It's a chance for you to give them the acknowledgment they deserve, and also provide them with an opportunity to inspire others.

Winners of recent awards or honors. These are the people who just won the big college scholarship, 4-H award, scouting honors, junior achievement, Citizen of the Month, etc. They may not be world famous, but they are highly credible experts and achievers — good, principled, unintimidating people whom your customers are likely to trust.

BECOME A CELEBRITY YOURSELF

One way to guarantee constant access to a celebrity and complete availability is to become one yourself. There are six basic ways to do this:

1. Organize and spearhead a fundraising drive for a worthy cause:

- Cancer research

- A refuge for abused women or children

- AIDS education

2. Do something for the community.

- Put together a recycling program that requires you to speak often to the media and other groups

- Organize an outreach program to the elderly that involves your product or service

3. Produce an event that brings people to town.

- A golf or other athletic tournament

- A statewide conference

4. Become an expert.

- You may not know any more than others in your field, but you probably know much more than the general population. "Experts" are those who have the courage and drive to stand forth and deliver that information in a public forum.

5. Create your own newspaper column or television/radio program.

- Start small (a monthly interview) and get bigger (a regular segment on a daily local talk show)

- Team up with your Walk Your Talk cross-promoting partner to author a weekly or monthly column in the local paper

6. Become active in your professional association.

- You are automatically an expert and minor celebrity if you're an officer of the plumber's union, the public relations association, the neighborhood retail council, or the garden supplies group. This may also be a good place to connect with Walk Your Talk cross-promoting partners.

HOW TO USE CELEBRITIES

Once you've caught a celebrity, what do you do with him or her? Again, the possibilities are limited only by your imagination. Here are some common ways that celebrities help promote organizations:

Endorsements that include a quote, photo, and/or signature on a sign in your office or store, in ads, or printed on the back of your receipt

Speaking at your demonstration or award celebration

Shaking hands with winners of your contests, especially if the announcement is made at your place of business

Signing autographs at your place of business and chatting with customers

Using their quotes about your product or service when you speak formally or informally

Appearing in educational audio or video tapes that feature your product or service, which are played in the store, given away, or mailed to press or potential customers.

A local football hero stars in a tape on literacy that is played continuously near the cash register at a video rental store. The tape both entertains and informs customers waiting to be checked out. Another alternative is to play these videos at eye level around the store so that people can watch while they shop or browse.

TREAT CELEBRITIES AS PARTNERS

Remember, your goals and the celebrity's goals for the event or promotion should be compatible and aligned — even if they're not exactly the same. You want to reach the same kinds of people. That is your common ground and common benefit. Make sure you both stay focused on producing that result, and that you both feel compensated in some way for your efforts.

Remember that celebrities are human beings; they don't like to feel used, and many of them don't like being put too high on a pedestal. Treat them as you would want to be treated, with respect and warmth. Let them know you appreciate their efforts on behalf of your product or service, and the cause you are both promoting.

SUMMARY

Endorsements by celebrities can be powerful, even when the celebrities are not world famous. Consider them your Walk Your Talk cross-promoting partners, <u>find ways for them to participate that produce the maximum results,</u> and make sure they know that you appreciate their contribution.

PRODUCE A
JOINT EVENT

Joint events are some of the most natural, exciting, and productive Walk Your Talk cross-promotions, perhaps because they bring you face-to-face with the reason you are cross-promoting — your customers. Events bring together your people, your partner's people, and also draw new people whom you both want to reach.

Joint events require planning and attention to detail, but they are fun, generate good media coverage, and are fairly simple to produce when you know exactly what results you want and follow the step-by-step plan in this chapter.

WHAT TYPE OF EVENT SHOULD YOU PRODUCE?

This is the first decision you and your partner must make. Your event should:

1. **Be manageable.** Always start small and work toward larger events.

2. **Target your audience specifically and directly.**

That leaves you a wide range of options. Some of the most successful joint events are:

Contests

Everybody loves contests. They create energy and excitement because they are a chance to show off talent or get lucky — and somebody always takes home a prize. Contests that are also Walk Your Talk cross-promotions should contain at least some of these elements:

1. They generate new enthusiasm in both your customers and your partner's current customers. Contests that are about new ways to sell and use your product or service may favor your regular customers, who know your organization best. Who can bring in the most new customers? Who can think of the most unusual way to use the product? To promote it? Who can come up with the best slogan, signature, or name for the new mascot?

"Frequent-user" contests are a great way to show your regular customers that you appreciate their support. These can be ongoing, or cover a week, month, or year.

Make your contest visible in both places of business with large or colorful coupons, displays, signs, and reminders from employees.

2. They let your customers know about your partner's organization, and his or her customers know about yours. Find a way to get your customers into your partner's store, and vice versa. People may have to get their raffle or entry tickets stamped at both of your places of business in order to win, or list which merchandise from each store they would select (with an upper price limit) if they won. Perhaps they have to fit together two halves of a ticket, or create some other winning combination of elements — one of which comes from your store and the other from your partner's.

3. They feature grand drawings or announcements of the winners. This generates enthusiasm and traffic, and may get press attention.

4. Ideally, the contest has something to do with the products or services you offer. A camera shop and framing store produced a photography contest and awarded equipment and framing as prizes. The next year, they were joined by a river rafting company for a contest featuring natural photography, and a river trip was added to the prizes.

The best contests are the ones that you and your partner think up in response to your specific needs and your customers' interests. They can be games of chance like drawings, prizes to reward talent, even fundraising competitions for worthy causes.

- Hastings clothiers in San Francisco chooses a Man and Woman of the Year who have raised the most money for the Leukemia Foundation. The Hastings Man and Woman are featured on billboards around town for two weeks wearing Hastings clothes, and the contest's supporting events include a fashion show M.C.'ed by local television celebrities, who also promote the contest on their shows.

- Merchants at a small local mall ran a contest to select sculptures by local artists. Cash prizes were awarded and the sculptures were displayed for a month.

Annual Street Fairs

These are Walk Your Talk cross-promotions among all the local merchants on the street, and have become increasingly popular and productive in recent years.

Fundraising Drives

Leading a fundraising drive for a popular or worthwhile cause — anything from cancer research to buying new band uniforms for the high school — always generates interest, good will, and generous publicity.

Free Noon-hour Lecture or Concert Series

These are becoming very popular in malls and downtown areas. People bring their lunch and sit outside, enjoying the lecture or concert. The talent is usually a Walk Your Talk cross-promoting partner working simply for the exposure. Signs and M.C.s let the audience know who is providing them with this free entertainment, and you may want to distribute discount coupons, introductory offers, or invitations to your current contest. You generate good will, new customers, and media attention — and make people smile in the bargain.

When the series is produced by multiple partners, as it often is at a mall, or when sponsored by a downtown business association, the partners can split up into teams with each team responsible for one day's lecture or concert. The deli and department store might present "Twelve Quick Meals" on Monday, the newspaper's movie critic and the video store team up for "Great Movies You May Have Missed" on Tuesday, and so on.

Neighborhood Days

Neighborhood merchants feature discounts and reductions, and promote the days or week with banners, signs, and specific color themes. You might, for instance, have everyone wear red clothes, arm bands, or pins, and key your decorations and promotional materials to that color.

"Time of Year" Events

These events aren't new — Back-to-School Days, Jump Into Spring, Easter on Main Street, Christmas tree lightings — but they are still effective and the variety of potential Walk Your Talk cross-promotional partners is almost unlimited.

- A dress boutique owner's annual "Moving Outside" spring fashion show is cross-promoted with seven other local businesses ranging from the hair stylist to the shoe store. To leverage visibility, the "Moving Outside" theme appears on a poster in every cooperating store's window. It is printed on all their receipts, featured on a handbill that customers get with their purchases, and promoted on door hangers placed on homes in the surrounding area.

- A ski shop owner sponsors a celebrity Ski Night at the beginning of each ski season. Championship racers discuss equipment and the best places to ski. A local radio station broadcasts live from the shop all day and the D.J. hosts the evening's entertainment. Walk Your Talk cross-promoting partners' shops get air time and use of the event's logo and publicity machinery. They also make their own goods and services available as raffle prizes. Listeners and shoppers can win catered picnics on the slopes, weekends at local resorts, snow tires, and entertainment passes.

Local Theme Events

What makes your community or area unique? Do you grow a certain crop — garlic, melons, artichokes — or produce a particularly succulent variety of sweet corn? Do you have a historical landmark or a connection to a famous person? What can you use as a theme to cross-promote your area with other organizations for a day, week, month, or year? If nothing comes to mind, can you make up a theme or tradition like "Put Centerville on the Map Week" or "Give a Dollar a Day to Your Favorite Charity Week"?

Educational Events

A fitness center might give free demonstrations for people who want to lose weight, who are pregnant or just had a child, or who are recovering from heart attacks. You give people information, which gets their attention and draws them to your place of business, and they have a chance to see and learn about your product or service.

These are only a few suggestions to stimulate your own creative ideas for events. Get together with your partner and brainstorm. You'll come up with something unique to your partnership, your community, and your customers.

MATCH THE EVENT TO YOUR PRODUCT OR SERVICE

Focus the event on what you and your partner do best. Stick to what you know, and tie in the event with your product or service. An aquarium store might not want to build an event around classical piano performances, for instance — unless their partner was the local symphony or piano retailer and they were planning to capitalize on the unusual partnership by placing huge aquariums around the stage.

Use humor whenever you can. A fitness center and a kitchenware shop teamed up for a "Divorce Special" event. Recently divorced people got discounts on gym memberships to get back in shape, and on kitchenware to restock their drawers and cabinets.

When you think about the people you want to draw, and about what you are offering them, events will start popping into your mind.

THE FOUR KEYS TO A SUCCESSFUL EVENT

You've pinpointed the audience you both want to reach. You've chosen an event that calls these people's attention to your organizations' special benefits. You believe the event will generate community interest and be something you can manage. Now what?

There are four keys to producing any event:

1. Establish a specific goal.

2. Plan your event and give it a "real-world" timetable.

3. Execute your plan.

4. Debrief with your partners.

The first and last steps are the ones most frequently overlooked, but they are crucial to producing a successful event.

1. ESTABLISH A SPECIFIC GOAL. This is your first and most important task; it determines everything else you do. Your goal should relate directly to reaching the specific market that you and your partner share.

Too often, partners don't take the time and energy to focus directly and specifically on what both of them want to achieve as a result of the event. They assume that they know where they are headed — toward a general goal of producing more business — but they never agree specifically (and in writing) on exactly what they want to accomplish.

When this happens, they often begin the process slightly out of step. Everything feels just a bit off. Even when the event goes fairly well, they don't feel a deep sense of accomplishment. They don't get the full satisfaction of moving from Point A to Point B, because they never completely defined Point B.

What are you really trying to accomplish by having this event? You may have primary and secondary goals, stated and unstated goals. A child care center, diaper service, children's toy store, children's clothing store, and hospital maternity ward may co-sponsor a "New Mother's Day" at the hospital, ostensibly to educate new mothers about resources and give them information about their new needs — yet among all these Walk Your Talk cross-promoting partners, there are a multiplicity of motivations.

The retail participants may support new mothers becoming well educated, but they also want to sell clothes, toys, clean diapers, and child care time — and also to reinforce their good image with existing clients by associating with educational programs. The hospital certainly has the new mothers' well-being in mind, but it also wants to encourage these women to use the hospital's others services.

It's important to sort out your primary and secondary goals, and to have your partner do the same.

Here are some possible goals for doing joint events, along with some ideas for events that would promote those goals:

A. Get current customers to use your product or service more frequently. Kick off a "frequent-user" contest for the summer that rewards your best customers with extra or free use of your product or service. Give the top three customers prizes from your Walk Your Talk cross-promotion partner's organization as well.

B. Gain visibility among potential new customers. These events target people who are not now using your product or service, but who might do so if they knew more about it:

- A clothing store opened their new children's department and made the first Saturday "Kids' Day," offering a 10% discount on all children's clothing. The store's Walk Your Talk cross-promoting partner was the PTA, which publicized its new literacy program in the store in return for letting parents know about the new department.

- A gas station informed potential customers of its expanded service department by giving free "Learn to Change a Tire" demonstrations on Sunday. Their partner was a women's aerobics center, which provided a service to members by letting them know about the tire-changing lessons and was listed as a co-sponsor — "brought to you by Ed's Chevron and Penny's Workout."

C. Reposition how the public sees your product or service. Do you want people to see you as more up-scale than you've been in the past, or as more "down home"? Do you want to let customers know that you've expanded to include fuller or better service, or that you've extended your hours? Celebrate your new direction with a sale week around your new up-scale or down-scale direction ("We're Moving

Up In the World" or "We're Letting Our Hair Down"). Throw a party and give discounts during the new hours.

D. Build a list of prospects. If your event's purpose is to generate a list of prospects, you need to get potential customers' names, addresses, phone numbers, and as much other information about them as possible. People are usually willing to tell you these things if they have a chance to win a prize or benefit in some other way, so drawings and raffles are particularly good ways to gather this information. These events involve minimal commitment from potential customers, and cost very little if you use your products or services as prizes.

E. Raise money and generate exposure for your nonprofit. When you set out to generate revenue, you can't be shy about asking people for money — whether you are the nonprofit itself or the Walk Your Talk cross-promoting partner. Your goal isn't merely to create good will toward your organization; you want them to like you *and* write a check.

Whether you produce a donation drive, an elegant dinner, an afternoon of wine-tasting, an auction, or any other fundraising activity, make sure that actually writing the check is an integral part of the function — or better yet, that the check is written **before** the event.

F. Recognize and reward your staff, and let your customers know that you appreciate the people who work for you. These events create a supportive corporate culture, motivate employees, and increase their loyalty, enthusiasm, and effectiveness. When you honor your staff in front of "strangers" — even if the "outsiders" are only your partner's staff — you make the recognition more public and give it more importance.

When you stand up to acknowledge people's efforts, be specific about what they have done. Give detailed testimonials that go beyond "most sales" or "best performance."

"Tony, the store manager, has been on the job only three months but has already demonstrated leadership and imagination with his new staff scheduling plan, his eye-catching product displays, and his coaching of clerks on how to approach customers when they come into the store."

"Cora, who has been under contract for five years to clean the store at night after closing, has responded to all your special requests and even offered her ideas about displays."

"Jason is the second newest salesperson, but he has lived up to his promise and drawn a whole new crowd of his younger peers into the store."

G. Reward your strongest clients and supporters. These events award prizes to people who have referred the most new customers, been coming to your place of business for the longest time, or used your product or service most.

Create events around these awards — in your place of business or at banquets outside your store — and find local "hooks" that ensure press coverage. Perhaps the people you honor are also long-time community volunteers, or great-grandmothers, or have some other unique characteristics that make them interesting to local readers, listeners, or viewers.

Your goal may be one of the above, or something entirely different. Talk with your partner about why you are producing the event, and try writing the joint purpose down in one sentence. Any lingering lack of clarity will emerge when you do that.

OUR PRIMARY GOAL IN PRODUCING THIS EVENT IS:

_____

_____

OUR SECONDARY GOALS ARE: _____

_____

_____

THE EVENT WE HAVE CHOSEN WILL ACCOMPLISH THESE GOALS BECAUSE:

_____

_____

When you are clear on your goals, then plan your event around them.

2. PLAN YOUR EVENT AND GIVE IT A "REAL-WORLD" TIMETABLE. The more specific your plans and your timetable, the better. Write down every small detail, every action you need to take in order to make your event work — then assign that action a realistic deadline and a person who is charge of making sure it happens. Build some fat into your schedule so that the sky doesn't fall in if something unexpected happens and a deadline is missed.

Your two most crucial planning tools are your **budget** and your **timetable**.

First, draft your budget. Include donated items and services with their approximate value so that donors feel appreciated and acknowledged.

Next, draft your timetable, starting with the five to ten biggest tasks.

Before you go any further, consult with your Walk Your Talk cross-promoting partners. Let everyone participate in filling in the details and creating the final version of both the budget and the time-table. Give your partners a chance to choose which tasks they will do and which they'd rather leave to you. Agree on everyone's responsi-bilities, tasks, costs, and deadlines. Make sure everyone has a copy of the budget and the timetable, and that you are all clear about both of these items.

Secure the location, as well as any related permits or approvals that you need from municipal or state agencies. Will the event be inside, outside on your own or your partners' property, or on public property? Will weather or temperature be of concern? What will you do if the weatherman doesn't cooperate?

Set the event schedule with a detailed list of everything that will happen during the event. Be specific. Plan what will happen during each quarter hour: when, where, how, and with whom. Walk through the schedule. Check out the physical space and consider the number of people involved. Will they be standing? Sitting? Do you have any special needs?

Consider worst-case scenarios. What are your legal, financial, and insurance needs? Ask your insurance agent about possible damage, personal injury, or other exposure that you might incur by doing the event, especially if it is outside, in a public or semi-public area, or involves any equipment (cars, rides, etc.). If you are raising money for a nonprofit through an outdoor event, you can get inexpensive insur-ance to cover your losses if you are rained out.

Consult the police department if parades are involved, the health department if food is involved, and the public works department if you are using any public facility. Your city council representatives can help you find the right city or county agencies to tell you if permits are required, or if plans must be reviewed.

Find new ways to draw people to your event. Review all five senses to consider all the ways you can attract people's attention and give them a reason to attend. What will they get to see, to touch, to taste, to smell, to hear, to do, or to take away? What will make their significant others want to come with them?

For instance, if you are doing a Saturday program on "The Complete Fisherman" at your sports shop that features a celebrity fisherman, new equipment, and outerwear, you might also have a travel agent in another part of your store to present "Great Four-day Romantic Getaways — With or Without Your Kids." That may help overcome possible resistance from spouses about their husbands running off to a "men's day" at your store during a family weekend.

Some classic ways to draw crowds are:

- **Giveaways:** food, product samples, such services as free introductory chiropractic diagnoses

- **Rides**

- **Demonstrations:** food, use of a new product, makeovers

- **Celebrities** lecturing, signing books or autographing equipment, being photographed with the crowd

- **Hands-on participation** and letting people do whatever is being promoted: video equipment, makeup, sports equipment

- **Surprise!** Announce prize winners or a new product.

- **Hobnobbing.** Make your event a chance to visit with friends, meet people your customers admire, or see figures they already know in new situations: politicians being dunked, high school student actors in ten-minute playlets they created, local television anchors in fashion makeovers.

Include in your budget, plan, and timetable everything you need to do to make your vision a reality. You may have hundreds of individual items. Assign responsibility for each one to someone in your Walk Your Talk cross-promoting partnership, and make sure everyone knows what everyone else is doing.

3. EXECUTE YOUR PLAN. Your plan may be simple or highly complex, but it should include at least the following:

Contact all the people involved in your event to schedule training and onsite practice, if necessary.

Plan your promotional material: cards, signs, ads, handbills, product bag enclosures, or whatever you and your partners have agreed to use. You will need materials to get the word out and generate enthusiasm prior to the event, and other materials for the event itself. How can you maximize your potential customers' exposure to your message? When, where, and to what kinds of messages will they be most receptive? Picture the space where the event will take place. Imagine how you can dramatize your message with high-impact signs, posters, and banners.

Design, print, copy, or draw your promotional material and props. Begin early to produce whatever you will need for your event so that if unexpected trouble arises, you won't get behind schedule.

Start distributing your promotional material. Mail your mailers, put up your signs, and start getting people enthusiastic about the event.

Gauge your estimated turnout. Consult with your partners to get a crowd estimate so that you can finalize your plans for food, space, seating, etc.

Do a dry run. Walk through every aspect of the event with your partners to make sure you all have the same idea in mind. Do this a few days beforehand, so that you have time to make adjustments if necessary. You might want to give your helpers and participants some social time to enjoy one another after this run-through. Take them out for pizza, or have food brought in.

Complete your "day-before-the-event" checklist. If you complete these tasks the day before, the event itself should go smoothly.

☐ Contact all participants to review and confirm what they are doing.

☐ Confirm that you have all the needed materials ready.

☐ Make a list of everything you must do the day of the event, in the order in which you must do them.

☐ Write similar task lists for other participants.

☐ Review these lists with your partners to make sure you haven't forgotten anything.

☐ Draft thank-you letters to everyone who helped with the event — from your partners to the most minor participant. Be specific in your praise, and also consider writing "third-party endorsement" letters to people who are important to your participants. These letters stress what wonderful people your participants are and what great jobs they did.

   For instance, write the radio station manager about the funny, thoughtful D.J. who plugged your event, or the parents of the student employee at your partner's business who pulled through when you needed help designing the promotional handbills.

   If you draft these letters the day before the event, you'll be ready to write the final versions and mail them quickly.

   Consider other forms of saying thank you as well, such as having a gift delivered to them when they are with people who are important to them: at work, in their school, at home, while they are at a civic club meeting. This not only feels good (to you and them), but also tells them that you're on their team, value your relationship with them, and want them to succeed. You show that you're a resourceful ally who gives a little extra.

The day of the event, begin your list of tasks. It's already organized, so you can go right down the list. Do each task at the earliest, not the latest, possible moment. Give yourself plenty of time to handle things that go wrong. Relax and enjoy yourself.

4. DEBRIEF WITH YOUR PARTNERS. Go over each aspect of the event to determine what worked and what didn't work. Take what I call the "childbirth" approach to debriefing. When a woman is giving birth, she doesn't look or feel radiant the entire time — but later she glows with happiness. Be willing to go through some discomfort to produce a good result.

Our inclination is to concentrate only on what went well and congratulate ourselves for how perfectly we performed, overlooking aspects of the event that might have been handled better. It's important to talk about the problems and the triumphs.

Hold the debriefing the day after the event while it is still fresh in everyone's mind. Focus first on what each of you want to do better or differently next time, and on what you could improve about the event. Then talk about what went well, congratulate one another, and give yourselves a big round of applause. Agree on the final bills, proceeds, mutual thank-you notes, and so on.

SUMMARY

Producing a joint event can be a fun, effective way to promote your organizations. Attention to detail, clarity about responsibilities, planning ahead, and keeping focused on your goals are the keys to success.

12

MAKE YOUR PLACE OF BUSINESS A LOCAL ATTRACTION

When you make your place of business a local attraction, people have more reason to come in and your traffic increases dramatically. You draw the people in your targeted market, and "hidden markets" may show up on your doorstep as well. You may attract people you didn't realize would be interested in your product or service.

Your organization may even become a place where people meet one another and gather socially, as malls have become. Those people are constantly exposed to your business or organization. If they so much as drink a cup of coffee, it's your coffee. You reach many more people, more often, in more interesting ways, with very little expense or effort.

When you cross-promote, you can create traffic *between* your places of business.

WHAT MAKES YOU A LOCAL ATTRACTION?

If you own the local fun park and ferris wheel, run the Chamber of Commerce Visitor Information office, or manage the fast food outlet with a thirty-foot hot dog out front, you are already a local attraction.

Local attractions are distinguished by something clever, unusual, visually striking, or uniquely valuable. People go out of their way to visit or pass by, and use the attraction as a meeting place, reference point, or landmark.

- "You know the thirty-foot hot dog? Turn left there." If the visitor is hungry, where will he or she eat before heading out of town?

- "I'll meet you in the electronics department at Mac's." Where else? Mac keeps six "demo" computers running all day long, filled to the gills with games.

There are an infinite number of ways to become a local attraction. What can you do to make people drop by, whether or not they plan to use your product or service? How can you capture their attention, pique their interest, stir their emotions, entertain their senses, or stimulate their minds? What can you do that is visually striking? How can you make your organization the place that *everybody* has to go next Saturday afternoon?

As you read the suggestions in this section, think of how you can use them with partners in Walk Your Talk cross-promotions. Also consider what you can do to create traffic *between* your places of business.

Here are a few ways to become an attraction in your community:

SIGNS: These are classic tools for promotion and advertising, but using them in clever or unusual ways can make you a local attraction.

- An equipment rental store in Honolulu maintains a huge signboard above its door using theater-marquee letters and pun-filled phrases like "Rug Shampooer Confesses: I Come Clean."

- State-of-the-art computerized billboards give people news and information, as well as messages about your product or service. People are drawn to the bright colors or flashing lights, as well as to these updates, and find themselves near your store or place of business just as your message moves across the screen.

Huge signs and billboards generate word-of-mouth publicity, one of the best kinds of free advertising — but there are two important rules if you go this route:

1. You must maintain a significant message and/or real humor week after week without fail.

2. You must be careful that your messages are never offensive. One Seattle automobile dealership may have crossed this line in 1980, when Iran held American embassy personnel hostage, by proclaiming on his billboard "Send the Shah back to Iran — strapped to a missile."

MOTTOES: When your motto becomes a local by-word, your place becomes a local attraction. Use your "signature phrase" ("We deliver" or "The fastest pizza in town") over and over — in all your promotional material, in advertising, and on large, attractive, or unusual banners in your place of business.

WINDOW DISPLAYS: It costs only imagination to make your windows so attractive, so clever, or so compelling that people make a special trip to see them. Many Chicagoans make an annual pilgrimage around Christmas to the Loop for the sole purpose of looking at Marshall Field & Company's department store windows.

In your nonholiday window displays, call attention to everyday local heroes and heroines. Feature photographs and a paragraph or two about people in your area who go out of their way to help others: a retired person who clears litter from a local park each week, or a child who returns a lost wallet to a tourist. Contact these people first for permission before you feature them, even if their stories have appeared in the newspaper or on television.

CONTESTS: Offer people something for nothing, and then stand back. Stage a drawing or offer prizes for the best motto for your store, for knowing the most trivia about your store's neighborhood, or for guessing the number of your (small) products in a jar. This "beans in a jar" contest can be a big draw if you get an extremely large jar and display it prominently in the store — or put it in your window.

VIDEOS: Videos always attract a crowd, especially when they are played on a large screen. You can either produce your own "infomercials" and "advertorials" promoting your product or service, or show related footage: sporting events, fashion shows, taped demonstrations of how to tie scarves in various ways, etc.

DOING GOOD: Volunteer your place of business as a "drop spot" for donations of food, clothing, or toys to worthy causes. You generate good will, become known as a socially responsible organization, and people have to come to your place of business to make their "drops."

INFORMATION: Set aside an area of your store for circulars on presentations at the library, schedules of civic events, neighborhood or area newspapers, and other information that is free and published on a regular basis. People will pop in at least once a week to pick up their copies, and you'll become a part of their lives.

If your organization caters to visitors and would benefit from tourist traffic, offer to print or distribute visitor information. Many tourist bureaus welcome "sponsorship" (advertisers) for maps and brochures. Ask your Chamber of Commerce about special maps that show businesses as local attractions.

Tourists on National City Guides tours in thirty-two cities hear advertisements for local businesses and organizations with their travelogues. "On your right is our historic bridge, and on your left is Gibson's Department Store." This keeps the cost of tours down and also promotes local businesses.

ANNUAL AWARDS: These are part of becoming well known in the community. Johnson's Camera Shop becomes more than just a store; it is the home of the Johnson Awards. People who live five hundred miles away may never have heard of the Johnson Awards, but that makes them even more important to locals, who have a better chance of winning and consider them "their own."

Make these awards memorable or clever, so that your organization is remembered for them the rest of the year. Try to connect them to your product or service.

• A music store and a piano teacher collaborated on a local version of the international music competition in Moscow.

• In the town where Smith's Hardware sponsors an annual building award for teens, high school students grow up thinking all year about the $2,500 Smith Award. That positive association sticks with many of them throughout their lives.

EVERYDAY PRODUCTS WITH YOUR LOGO ON THEM: A special store at Apple Computer headquarters sells sweatshirts, T-shirts, coffee mugs, and jewelry with the Apple logo on them. Coca-Cola offers a line of logo-decorated shirts, towels, and other items to clothing stores around the world, and has even opened its own retail outlet.

You can produce attractive but inexpensive caps, T-shirts, and sweatshirts with your name and logo, and make them available at low prices in your store. Each time someone steps out onto the street wearing one, you get free advertising and become more of a local attraction.

EVENTS: If an event is held at your place of business, everyone who hears about the event also hears about you. The event's appeal and importance rubs off on you, whether or not you have anything to do with producing it.

One of the hottest new events is the shopping mall concert, but you don't need a shopping mall location to sponsor one of these engaging performances. You may just need a parking lot, or access to the sidewalk outside your store or your partner's place of business.

Performers — whether they are a high school rock band, a young soprano, or a barbershop quartet — get exposure and/ or donations from passers-by. You get a crowd outside your business, and become a local-attraction-for-a-day. Find a way to bring people inside after they've listened for a while — with signs, contests, or other promotions.

If you are located in a mall, the other merchants are your natural Walk Your Talk cross-promoting partners and you can stage a larger production. One California mall premiered a new rock act called the Boys Club over President's Day weekend before throngs of breathless teenage girls who had never before touched a live rock star and loved the fact that the Boys Club were "like totally" accessible to them. The girls brought thousands of extra dollars to mall merchants, and the Boys Club sold hundreds of its new album. As is the case with most Walk Your Talk cross-promotions, everybody won: the Boys Club, the mall merchants, and the girls.

DO THE UNUSUAL: Anything unusual attracts attention. Dream up Walk Your Talk cross-promotions that are unusual enough to make people look twice, but not so unusual that you seem weird to the people you're trying to attract.

- A restaurant in San Francisco serves free wine or sparkling water to people waiting to dine. Another popular restaurant hires a magician to entertain those waiting to be seated on Friday and Saturday nights.

- Placing your product in an unusual place can make it an attraction. VideoRated, Inc. in Costa Mesa puts videotape rental vending machines in hotel lobbies and tape players in Best Western, Super 8, and Image Inn hotel rooms. Vending machines hold fifty to two hundred tapes, which can be rented with major credit cards.

No matter what you do to make your place of business a local attraction, be sure that people know how to find you. Include maps in your promotional material if possible, or make your location part of your message: "Smith's Hardware, at the corner of First and Main."

THE "DOUBLEMINT STRATEGY"

Teaming up with other merchants and organizations in related fields, or in close proximity to you, is not only good Walk Your Talk cross-promoting; it is one of the best ways to draw traffic. You make your *group* the local attraction.

Twins in Doublemint chewing gum ads exhorted viewers to "double your pleasure." When organizations in related fields share locations and promotions, they can double their exposure, customers, and profits.

This new phenomenon is sometimes known as the "specialty mall" and features many businesses involved in one field — home improvement, health and beauty, auto care — clustered together in one geographic location which becomes a local attraction.

The "auto mall" is a perfect example. In these "car-care centers," all the businesses are car-related: mechanics, tire dealerships, gas stations, car washes, detail and repair shops, car stereos and accessory stores, cellular phone and burglar alarm outlets, and franchised muffler, transmissions, tune-up, and brake businesses. Each draws its own customers, who usually find it convenient to do some other auto-related business with neighboring dealers as well.

The specialty mall is the wave of the future, because everybody wins. Customers get convenience, and merchants get more business. People buy the new tire or car stereo that they would have postponed because they're already at the auto mall to get the car washed — especially if the carwash is a good cross-promoter and has large signs advertising specials on new tires or stereos. This kind of synergy can generate as much as 15% of a shop's annual business. Dealers cash in on one another's customers, enjoy heavy traffic, and slash costs with

Walk Your Talk cross-promotions and joint advertising for the mall as a whole.

Home improvement stores are also starting to use the "Doublemint strategy." These malls attract home builders and do-it-yourself homeowners. They feature outlets for lumber, paint, tile, carpeting, plumbing fixtures, electronics, tools, lighting, etc.

"Food courts" of ten to thirty outlets clustered together within larger shopping malls are another use of the "Doublemint strategy" to create local attractions.

Even when only two or three similar businesses combine forces, they become more of an attraction.

- In Cheyenne, Wyoming, Bresler's 33 Flavors Ice Cream Parlor occupies 700 square feet of the 3,200-square-foot Taco John facility.

- An Everything Yogurt shop divided its 500-square-foot mall space into two parts and teamed up with Bananas, which sells "frosty fruit shakes." Total sales for the two enterprises rose 25-30%, and profits were up even more because both businesses saved on rent and promotional costs.

The "Doublemint strategy" works another way as well. Many businesses find that they become a local attraction **because they are different, but share the same physical space.** This arrangement also provides customer convenience.

- Video kiosks are starting to appear in Safeway, Sears, and other stores.

- Automatic teller machine customers in Los Angeles, Philadelphia, New York, and Washington, D.C., can now obtain Amtrak tickets from their ATM.

- Gas stations are becoming one-stop shopping centers where you can fill up your tank; pick up fresh doughnuts, pizza, and bread; buy a lottery ticket; copy documents; rent a video; buy balloons; order hamburgers and fries; and pick up a fistful of trading stamps — all in a highly visible drive-by location.

- Truck stops are also becoming centers for shopping and living. The industry's newest complexes boast movie theaters, restaurants with phones at every table, fax machines, showers for couples, television rooms, washer/dryers, and chiropractors for aching backs. One facility in Florence, South Carolina, even has a hair salon where truckers can get their hair styled, cut, and colored.

- Attracted by a captive market of cash-hungry consumers, many banks have begun offering full-service branches in supermarkets, and customers are taking home certificates of deposit, car loans, and checking accounts along with their Cornflakes and Cheez Whiz. "It's just begun to catch fire," says Thomas Garrott, President of the Memphis-based National Bank of Commerce. His bank has opened thirty-three of its forty-eight branches in Tennessee in Kroger supermarkets.

  Most branches are strategically positioned near check-out stands and feature big, bright signs advertising no-fee credit cards or same-day loan approval. These aggressive marketing tactics are meant to challenge the traditional image of bankers in pin-striped suits. In the increasingly fierce battle for customers, banks have to show that they can offer better service and convenience than their competitors. Supermarket branches offer longer banking hours, the ease of one-stop shopping, and homey touches.

  "Rather than positioning ourselves like a bank, we are acting more like grocery merchants," says Garrott. That means trying to generate a high volume of low-cost transactions, like opening checking accounts.

Use the "Doublemint strategy" to your advantage. Businesses are moving closer together in geographic clusters that automatically become local attractions because they offer customer convenience. Work with the organizations near you — whether they are in your field or wildly diverse — to take advantage of this natural opportunity to cross-promote. Make your block or your neighborhood a local attraction by creating a team that supports one another and generates enthusiasm throughout your community.

SUMMARY

Making your place of business a local attraction is a foolproof way to generate traffic, sales, and usage. A little imagination goes a long way, and you're ahead of the game if you work with the people who are close to you geographically.

CHAPTER 13

SPEAK OUT: A GUIDE TO MAKING GREAT SPEECHES (AND GETTING INVITED TO DO SO)

<u>Speaking is another promotional tool that costs you virtually nothing,</u> provides a service to your customers and your community, gives you high visibility and outreach, and may establish you as an expert who is called for quotes, opinions, and background information when news breaks in your field.

Speaking also lets you target your market very specifically. You usually know exactly who will be in your audience.

When you cross-promote with a partner, speaking becomes an even more powerful strategy.

SPEAKING WITH YOUR PARTNER

If you speak together, you can "piggy-back" on one another's subjects, contacts, energy, and invitations — and two speakers often make a more dramatic presentation than one. You may even be able to interact and play off one another — whether in a light, comedic fashion or in a mock-adversarial, point/counterpoint style — providing entertainment as well as information and making your speaking duo even more attractive to a wider audience.

You may also get a better response if you speak together. You draw both of your individual audiences, and offer two areas of expertise instead of one. New people are more likely to show up because they are getting a double return on their investment of time. Putting your two subjects together may also make each topic more interesting than it was by itself. Speaking together can also make it easier to walk up to the front of the room.

If you sell computer software and your partner is in the office supply business, for example, the two of you could put together an interesting, valuable, and even humorous presentation on how computers don't mean the death of office supplies and how people can let the two systems support one another.

You could make this presentation on radio or local television, to practically any business organization, and even to your respective professional associations. It's also a speech that might get media coverage because of its general appeal.

You and your partner don't have to be stand-up comics or presidential-caliber speakers. To make an impact and become known as sources of information, you just have to talk about what you know and make your expertise available to others.

CHOOSING YOUR SUBJECT

First, choose a topic for your speech. Begin with your mutual markets. Whom do you want to reach? What topics interest those people?

Brainstorm with your partner to find ideas, and write them all down. You'll start with only one speech, but you may want to expand your repertoire later, so save these valuable ideas.

Choose a subject that leaves people with a positive impression of you, but that also entertains and informs. Be clear about what you want to say, and about the result you want to produce. Try not to sound like a commercial or roll over people with a "hard sell."

Remember: **A good speech — like a good product or service — defines a need and fills it**.

Ask your current customers what kind of speech would interest them, and what kinds of information they want or need. Write down the questions that they ask you most often. A pet store owner wrote down the questions she was asked most often and put together a twenty-minute presentation that answered them all in an amusing way. One of her customers told his veterinarian about her, and now the pet store owner and the vet cross-promote by speaking together in their own "dog and pony show."

A toy store owner who had studied child development used questions from parents to shape her speech around ten educational toys, showing how each could help children learn language. Later, she began speaking with a professor from the local university's child development program, who gave her more credibility while he found new clients for the department's ongoing research projects.

Your goal in speaking should be to meet new people and give them something of value. They will respond later by patronizing your business, mentioning you to their friends and colleagues, and generating new speaking offers for you.

WHERE SHOULD YOU SPEAK?

Target some specific places or events where you will reach the most customers and potential customers most effectively. Where do the people you want to reach get their information? Where do they get their entertainment? Those are the places you want to be.

Good places to give talks include:

- Civic groups with an educational bent

- M.C.'ing a civic or nonprofit event

- Bookstores

- Demonstrations in your place of business, or your partner's

- Radio call-in "talk-to-an-expert" shows

- Five-minute interviews

- Local or cable television educational programs

- Introducing someone else at one of these places

Make a list of five places your customers get their news and entertainment. How can you reach those media with your speech? Start small, then speak to larger or more challenging audiences as you develop confidence.

GETTING INVITED TO SPEAK

Good speakers are always in demand, and groups that present programs on a regular basis are constantly on the lookout for new and interesting speakers and topics — but you have to let these people know that you are available. Don't be afraid to contact:

- Program chairs of civic and professional associations

- Radio and television producers

- Local clubs and fraternal organizations

- Bookstore owners

Make an appointment to see these people, and ask them about their needs. What kind of speakers do they use? How often do they use speakers? What do their audiences want to hear? Then tell them what you have to offer — your expertise, your experience, the points on which you can speak — and find out how you can best work together.

When you call, they may want you to send a letter outlining this information, along with a photo or videotape, before they meet with you.

WRITING YOUR SPEECH

Do research to make your talk the best that it can be. You may want to include:

- Interesting information about the history of your product: housewares, pet care items, children's clothing, gasoline, picture framing, graphic arts, psychology, technical writing, sandwiches, restaurants, etc.

- What is happening on the cutting edge of your industry?

- What are we likely to see in your field fifty years from now?

- What is the strongest impact that your industry, or your product or service, is having on people's lives today? How is that affecting the members of your audience's lives right now?

Start a file for interesting bits of information that you run across and may want to use later in a speech. Before each speech, check this file for new items and add them if appropriate. This keeps your speeches fresh and current.

Everything you say will either strengthen or detract from your message. Don't waste your energy or scatter your audience's attention by trying to "fill up time." Say only what is important, then stop. It's okay to be brief.

If you are unaccustomed to writing, put down your best points and examples on index cards. Place all the cards on a table in random order and move them around until you find an organization that makes sense to you. Write as many drafts of your speech as you feel is necessary.

Some good elements to include are:

1. Funny, poignant, unusual, startling, or heartwarming incidents that happened to you or your customers in the store

2. Quotes from people your audience knows and admires

3. Informative or amazing statistics

4. Cartoons, illustrations, and photographs — be visual whenever possible

5. Props (samples of your product, tools or supplies you use, etc.), especially if they are not often seen by the public

6. Facts about your host, your audience, or the site or surroundings where you are speaking

The final test for whether your speech is ready to deliver is this: is it something you would enjoy or benefit from hearing yourself?

PREPARING YOURSELF

Practice your speech aloud. Try it out on friends and family, and ask them for feedback. Friends and family aren't usually critical enough, but any feedback is better than none.

Remember why you are giving the speech: to get the word out about your product or service. Focus on your message, and on extending yourself to your audience. This gives you something to occupy your mind and keeps your attention off yourself. It keeps you centered and on target, even when butterflies begin.

You are not giving the speech in order to become crazy or nervous, or to have a bad time. Relax, and concentrate on what you are saying. Speak to the audience as you would talk to people in your place of business. Enjoy yourself.

Before you speak, anticipate the best and worst that could happen. Imagine how you would handle disasters like the microphone not working or difficult people in the audience. Then take a deep breath, and imagine the best that could happen. Close your eyes and watch a mental "movie" of the speech from beginning to end, just as you want it to occur. Replay this tape several times, and once more before you actually speak.

MEMORABLE HANDOUTS AND GIVEAWAYS

Your words will have more impact and linger longer if people take away a written version or amplification of your speech. Give your audience a flyer, brochure, or other handout either before or after your speech.

If the handout is particularly helpful or interesting, your audience may even pass it around to their friends and colleagues. You can also give it to reporters as background for radio, television, or newspaper interviews. This handout may be something you can give to your customers as well.

If you distribute the handout before your speech, make it something to which they will need to refer while you are speaking. Otherwise, it becomes a distraction. They will be reading it while they should be listening to you.

Include in your handout:

1. The title of your speech

2. Your name and the name of your organization, its address, phone number, hours, and directions to its location, if necessary

3. A brief description of yourself and your business

4. The points you made in your speech, or the tips you passed along

5. A list of resources (publications and organizations) that can provide related information, products, or services

6. An illustration, photograph, or other visual element that "shows, not tells" your points

The kitchenware shop owner, who became a professional speaker after the success of her "Five Gourmet Meals You Can Make in 30 Minutes" speech, distributed a handout that did not parrot what she said. Instead, it expanded on one aspect of the speech. She gave her handout the dramatic title "Unexpectedly Romantic Evenings for Two" and included, in addition to three delicious recipes:

- Tips to make any meal special, such as using scented candles

- A picture of herself giving a cooking demonstration in her store to three local celebrities: a quarterback, a socialite, and a business leader

- A list of thirty items to keep on hand for making romantic meals on short notice

- A list of stores (including her own) that carried those items

SUMMARY

Speaking can be rewarding, as well as productive and profitable. Using speaking as an ongoing Walk Your Talk cross-promotion with your partner can be even more fun and reach even more people. Remember that your purpose is to deliver a message about your product or service, but that you must also inform and entertain your audience. Prepare carefully, then relax and enjoy yourself — so that your audience can relax and enjoy themselves.

CHAPTER 14

JUMP-START CUSTOMER SERVICE

Customer service can be your strongest, least expensive promotional tool. There is no better way to keep your customers coming back, and telling their friends about you, than to give them more for their money in a way that makes them feel good about themselves.

When you cross-promote, you can work together to improve and expand customer service. Your partnership is based on working with the same kinds of people; make yourselves experts at serving that particular market.

CUSTOMER SERVICE CAN MAKE, OR BREAK, A BUSINESS

Customer service has a greater impact on your business — for better or worse — than any other factor. People should be smiling each time they leave your store, and everyone in your organization should be aware of these four facts:

1. **People are more likely to stop doing business with you because of poor customer service than for any other reason.** One of your sales clerks is talking on the phone and sees a customer approaching. Instead of hanging up and asking what she can do to help, she turns her back on the customer and continues her conversation. This is the fastest, and one of the most common, ways that organizations lose business, according to "Mystery Shopper" and customer service consultant Kay Hollenbeck. Another sure-fire disaster is for clerks to start helping customers, then get distracted and never return.

Sit down with a pad of paper and write for thirty minutes about your worst experiences as a customer. Include interactions with retail businesses, service organizations, and government agencies. Next to each experience, write down how you felt and the opinion you formed about that business or organization as a result.

2. **Customers are willing to pay up to 10% more for your product or service if they know they will receive "outstanding customer service."** They have enough stress in their lives without being treated rudely by an organization to which they are paying good money, and they are too busy to spend time straightening out messes. If you can save them time or aggravation, they are glad to pay you a little more and will choose you over a competitor who doesn't provide great customer service — even if the competitor's product or service is the same and his prices are lower.

3. **Customers who are happy about your excellent service are your best, and least expensive, source of advertising.** Not only do current customers bring you more business, they bring you better business. These new customers arrive prepared to like your product or service, and to tell *their* friends. On average, each satisfied customer

will recruit five additional customers for your business. Each unhappy customer will tell *seven* people about his or her experience.

"Any business lives by word-of-mouth," says William Davidow, co-author of *Total Customer Service* (Harper & Row, 1989), "and for a small business that can't afford other kinds of promotion, word-of-mouth is a life-and-death factor." He says that if you are a small business, you should ask your best customers to describe exactly what kinds of service they expect. Then ask the customers if they recommend your organization to others. If they don't, find out why.

4. **Customers' perceptions of your business are shaped more by the quality of your service than by the quality or cost of your products.** Many consumers believe that customer service is part of what they are buying. They are afraid to buy from an organization that's known for shoddy customer service, and willing to overlook other problems if you have a good reputation for customer service.

For many products, including computers and electronics, people say, "I don't care so much about the price; I want to know that someone can tell me what to do if I get stuck and that they'll fix it if something goes wrong."

Paying attention to customer service may have saved The Good Guys, Inc., when it was just a small northern California consumer electronics chain with giant Circuit City stores nipping at its heels. Good Guys founder and President Ronald A. Unkefer re-examined his business and concluded that California customers hated haggling over price, which was common practice in the consumer electronics field at that time. He outlawed haggling and adopted a more genteel approach: 15% lower prices and a guarantee to match any competitor's price. He also improved staff training and stepped up advertising. The tactic worked because he gave customers what they wanted.

CUSTOMER SERVICE WITH A PARTNER

Working together with a partner makes almost everything you do easier and less expensive, including taking customer service to new heights in both of your organizations. You know who your customers are and are serving the same kinds of people, so you can share training

196 ■ WALK YOUR TALK

costs and create joint programs that generate double enthusiasm among your staffs.

Here are some ways that Walk Your Talk cross-promoting partners can support one another in improving customer service:

1. Brainstorm about new customer service ideas. Your partner may see something that you could be doing, and you may see something that he or she could be doing.

2. Hold joint customer service trainings for your staffs. These are also a chance for your staffs to meet and get to know one another, which makes them all better cross-promoters.

3. Offer joint incentives to your staffs for good customer service. The prizes might be one another's products and services, which is another way to stimulate Walk Your Talk cross-promotion because both staffs become more familiar with what the other does.

4. Send both staffs to workshops that improve the way they connect with customers. You might even get a discount for sending more people, and this is another chance for your staffs to spend time together.

5. Make Walk Your Talk cross-promoting part of your customer service. Recommendations and cross-referrals flow naturally between two Walk Your Talk cross-promoting partners who are genuinely interested in customer service and believe in one another's products:

- Jerry's Doughnut Shop cross-promotes with Alice's Auto Repair. Although these two businesses offer vastly different products, they serve the same market because they are in the same block. Both staffs benefited from a joint customer service training that covered friendliness and courtesy (smiling and remembering people's names), attitudes (the customer is always right), and maximizing sales ("Would you like a cup of coffee with that doughnut, Mr. Smith?" "Shall we check the brakes, too, Mrs. Smith?"). When Nadine the Honda specialist suggests that people pass the time at Jerry's Doughnut Shop while waiting for their smog checks, she can now ask them with genuine enthusiasm to say hello to Arnold, whose specialty is cream puffs.

- Veterinarian David Samuels cross-promotes with The Cat's Pajamas Pet Shop, and they have become a part of his customer service. When his client Betty called about Fluffy's fleas, he referred her to The Cat's Pajamas, saying, "Try spraying her at home with a new product that's just come out, and if that doesn't work we'll give her a flea bath here. I'll call Joe at The Cat's Pajamas and tell him to have some waiting for you."

- You can also offer discounts at one another's organizations as part of your customer service. Your tire outlet might provide discounts at the carwash, and the carwash offer discounts on your tires. Lingerie and bath shops might offer the same kinds of reciprocal discounts.

WHAT DO PEOPLE WANT?

What kinds of customer service are most important to people? The best way to discover people's specific wants and needs is to ask them. Find out directly from your customers what you can do to serve them better. As long as you're investing time, energy, and possibly money in customer service, you might as well target the areas that will produce the best feelings and the strongest results.

Poll your customers, and ask them what specific improvements they'd like to see. Would different store hours be more convenient? What about delivery? What would make them use your product or service more often? Find out what they don't like as well, and make whatever changes you can.

Even franchises can individualize service to suit local needs and tastes. McDonald's outlets serve "saimin" (noodle soup) in Hawaii, wine in France, and beer in Germany. The Arby's roast beef sandwich franchise in South Portland, Maine, offers locally grown asparagus, crab and lobster sandwiches, and homemade salad dressings.

Ask your customers how you can make their lives easier, and find your own creative ways to go the extra mile for their business.

THANK PEOPLE FOR DOING BUSINESS WITH YOU

Everybody wants to feel appreciated, and thanking people who use your product or service is a fundamental of good customer service. Here are some ways to do that:

1. Offer "frequent-user" coupons, discounts, and other incentives.

2. Give them "first crack" at a huge sale. Open the store a few hours early and let them have first choice of the bargains.

3. Write "thank-you" letters to steady customers, and perhaps enclose information on products related to those they buy.

4. Offer these related products at such low prices that they can't refuse.

5. Give them small gifts or presents: pencils, calendars, buttons with the store name, refrigerator magnets, or product samples.

Your "thank you" doesn't have to be elaborate; the gesture is what counts. A very small gift or discount goes a long way when they know that you genuinely appreciate them and their business.

You can cross-promote at the same time that you reward your customers by offering them samples or discounts on your partner's product or service.

Give your current customers a reason to tell their friends about your organization, and your partner's.

TEN QUICK TIPS FOR PERSONALIZING CUSTOMER SERVICE

Offering extra service doesn't necessarily mean hiring new people or rethinking your marketing plan. Here are ten quick, free or inexpensive ideas for jump-starting customer service and making it more personal:

1. Get to know regular customers' names.

2. Encourage customers to fill out suggestion forms, and make those forms readily available.

3. Follow up on all suggestions with hand-signed thank-you notes.

4. Offer regular customers the convenience of a house charge account.

5. Establish company policies that honor all reasonable requests for product returns and refunds.

6. Answer telephones promptly and courteously.

7. Use the telephone as a marketing tool. Reach out to your customers and let them know personally about sales and other promotional events.

8. Offer convenience services, such as extended hours or free delivery.

9. Send birthday cards to customers and offer them a 10% discount if they come in with the card.

10. Mail your customers a monthly newsletter or catalog announcing specials, new products or services, and events at your place of business.

EMPLOYEES ARE THE HEART OF YOUR CUSTOMER SERVICE

Employees are the people who deliver your customer service. All that people know about you, they experience through your staff. Everything your employees do and say should communicate that they care about their customers. Anything less says that they don't.

- A visitor to Dallas' Sewell Village Cadillac who owned a retail store in Connecticut said after a tour, "They love what they're doing. You can't fake a positive attitude like the one they have. I even saw it in the guy who was sweeping the floor."

    Sewell Village has a sign over the service department that proclaims: "We reserve the right to give preferential treatment to those who purchase their automobile from Sewell Village Cadillac." They provide new car buyers with a personal service representative who writes up all of that customer's service orders, answers his or her questions and complaints, and arranges for emergency road service. They make their showroom an inviting place with fresh flowers, brass chandeliers, and uphostered furniture. Visitors and even competitors are allowed to tour the service department, which is the largest in the country. Sewell is the second-highest rated Cadillac dealer nationwide in customer satisfaction.

    Service Director Philip Dunnet says, "Our service department really becomes another sales department. We have customers who might hate their goddamn car, but they don't want to lose their service guy, so they come back and shop with us. Basically, we attempt to take the automobile out of the deal altogether, and put a person in its place."

- One California bank wants its employees to impress customers with "the speed and consistency characteristics of McDonald's and the personal attention for which Nordstrom's is known." The bank is making "personal bankers" out of its employees, urging them to keep their desktops free of clutter for a more professional image and generally focusing on the "retail" side of banking. Branches will stay open longer, up to twelve hours a day in some locations, and employees will be expected to dress more like the executives they want for customers.

GIVE YOUR STAFF A GREAT SCRIPT

Help your employees provide great service. Make sure they know exactly what is expected of them — in terms of attitudes, courtesies, and policies toward customers — and that they have the tools to carry out those tasks.

Good customer service starts with a good script. Imagine that your customers' interactions with you are a series of scenes that form a play. The play is about making them happy with you and enthusiastic about your product or service. What should happen in the beginning? The middle? The end? Who are the players and what are their parts?

Create a storyboard, beginning when customers enter your place of business. How should they be greeted? What should your staff's attitude be? How should customers feel? What can your employees do to make them feel that way? Take customers through their whole interaction with your organization, then visualize the final sales. Next, take them through many years of outstanding customer service and spreading the word about your organization among friends.

To play their part in this drama, your staff need a script. Tell them how to greet customers, what kind of atmosphere to create, and how to treat your "guests." This script isn't a series of words that they will memorize, although you might give them some suggestions about how to approach customers, move them through objections, close sales, and deal with them in the long term. Rather, your script describes an environment you want to create for your customers. It might include a calmed, relaxed atmosphere, personal attention, or quick and convenient service.

Tell your employees what Walt Disney's management tells theirs: When you are with customers, you are on stage. Your job is to play your part the way it is written. Everything else should be handled "backstage" — at home, in the employee lounge, or in the manager's office. Nothing should interfere with the customers' positive experience of your organization.

Your ultimate goal should be to provide customers with an experience that exceeds their expectations.

BE INNOVATIVE

Always be ready to respond to customers' changing needs, and don't be afraid to try the unusual.

- Aaron Montgomery Ward's catalogue was really just an innovation in customer service, but it revolutionized marketing in America. In the 1870s, Ward discovered that rural Americans wanted to buy the same goods that urban dwellers did, but often could not afford to travel to cities. His way of improving customer service was to publish a catalogue offering comparable merchandise at low prices. He guaranteed customer satisfaction in order to overcome people's initial resistance to buying goods sight-unseen from strangers, and also gave Grange members ten days' credit. By 1884, annual sales had reached $1 million, and by 1913, they were up to $40 million, with some six thousand employees to handle the business. Sears Roebuck & Co. followed suit, and later became even more successful than Ward's company. Both had the vision and daring to serve customers in a new way.

- Hotels and motels often offer quirky incentives to lure guests when business is slow. The Anderson House in Wabasha, Minnesota, offers cats for overnight adoption to people who miss their own pets. Yellow rubber ducks are found in all the bathtubs at the McLean, Virginia, Hilton. The Amish Dinner Package at the Intercourse, Pennsylvania, Best Western Motel Village Inn offers patrons a two-night motel stay, a two-hour tour of the Amish country, and one dinner in the home of a real Amish family.

MAKE YOURSELF MOBILE

It's easier for people to do business with you if you come to them, or if you offer free or inexpensive pick-up and delivery. This isn't possible for every organization, but at least think about the possibilities. Convenience can make all the difference, especially in highly competitive businesses.

- Many independent fast food outlets deliver ribs, chicken, burgers, fish, and even cold beer to customers in return for a minimum order or a small fee.

- The Grocery Express in San Francisco calls itself "The All-Delivery Market." Customers don't come in; they telephone their orders from a free catalogue. The Grocery Express even takes orders by fax. They are adept at the art of soliciting testimonials, one of the many rewards of superior customer service. "Never again will I step inside a grocery store!" said a busy executive who typified the kind of customer Grocery Express wants. "With Grocery Express, I don't wait in long lines, maneuver crowded aisles to tote heavy bags. Give them a call and you too will become spoiled as I have over the past four years."

- Qualified mechanics who pick up cars for repairs, tune-ups, or detailing — and return them quickly — find that their businesses expand quickly.

- Private veterinary "ambulances" can double as pick-up and delivery vans for nonemergency pet visits. Mobile veterinary hospitals make it easier for pets to get regular checkups.

- Even such giants as IBM are paying heed. To provide greater convenience for his rural customers, an IBM sales representative in North Carolina created a portable showroom, "The Solution Mobile," by filling a mobile home with computer equipment and visiting customers in their homes or businesses.

GO THE EXTRA MILE

One way to go the extra mile is to stay open extra hours, even if you only have a skeleton staff. With almost everyone working out of the home, it's not as easy to shop or get services during the day as it was twenty years ago.

Saving time is one of the most attractive benefits you can offer customers these days. Lens Crafters and others cash in on their ability to get people in and out in one hour.

"Society has broken from the boundaries of daytime," says Murray Melbin, a sociologist at Boston University, in *Night as Frontier: Colonizing the World After Dark* (Free Press, 1987). He notes that most service businesses are now open at night, including brokerage houses, factories, and gas stations. We now have twenty-four-hour data processing centers, maintenance companies, and crisis clinics. He cites research showing that some twenty-nine million Americans are awake at midnight, and that ten million are active between 3:00 and 5:00 PM — most of them at work.

Going the extra mile with customer service can be more valuable to your organization than advertising. Gelson's Century City 7 supermarket in Beverly Hills thrives although it buys no ads, prints few coupons, and keeps prices high. The meat department is self-service but there are nineteen workers on hand to help. Manager Dennis Holran says, "What we offer is service, quality, and cleanliness."

THE TEN COMMANDMENTS OF GREAT CUSTOMER SERVICE

When in doubt, or whenever you want to jump-start customer service or move it to a new level, follow these ten commandments:

1. Ask your best customers to tell you honestly what kind of service they expect from your organization.

2. Establish clear and simple service policies to match your customers' expectations.

3. Give authority to people at every level of your organization so that they feel empowered to provide good service.

4. Eliminate all red tape involved in merchandise returns.

5. Set clear customer service goals for your employees and make sure that everyone understands them.

6. Provide specific information and training so that employees know exactly what to do in every situation.

7. Write clear job descriptions for every employee that include customer service, and offer incentives for promotion so that people don't feel stuck in dead-end jobs. Their attitudes will be apparent to customers.

8. Make employees accountable for their actions, especially in the arena of customer service.

9. Publicly reward and recognize your employees for good customer service.

10. If you can't hire an outside firm to analyze and critique your customer service, ask your friends or neighbors to visit your organization and report on the service they receive.

SUMMARY

Customer service can make or break your organization. Use great service to reward current customers, keep them coming back, and turn them into salespeople, as well as to attract new customers. Ask your customers what they want in terms of service, and make it easy for your staff to provide those things. Keep in constant touch with both your customers and your staff about how to improve customer service. It's one of your best promotional tools, and can be absolutely free.

Use your Walk Your Talk cross-promoting partnership to enhance customer service by sharing staff training and perhaps offering one another's product or service as an incentive or reward.

CHAPTER

15

BE CREATIVE: UNUSUAL ADVERTISING MEDIA

<u>Creativity is the fuel that runs Walk Your Talk cross-promotion at the local level</u>. Walk Your Talk cross-promotion itself is an innovative concept, especially when it involves crossing the lines among business, nonprofits, and government. Bring that creative, pioneering spirit to your search for media in which to promote your products or services.

LOOK OUTSIDE THE NINE DOTS

Can you connect all the dots in this puzzle using only four straight lines, without ever lifting your pen from the paper?

```
 •   •   •

 •   •   •

 •   •   •
```

The solution surprises many people because they have to go outside the nine dots:

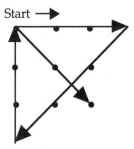

To solve this puzzle, you have to look at it in an unusual and innovative way. Don't forget to look "outside the nine dots" when you consider ways to cross-promote your products or services.

BREAK THE MOLD

King Camp Gillette founded an industry by going outside the nine dots. Gillette had been a sales representative for a company that made disposable bottle stoppers in the late 1800s. The company's owner often encouraged Gillette to develop products "that could be used and then thrown away."

By 1903, Gillette had begun to sell a unique razor with disposable blades that was considered a mere novelty at first — but Gillette priced the blades so low that, as one historian put it, "parsimony became unnecessary." The safety razor became a great success among soldiers and sailors during World War I, and they refused to give it up after the war was over. Disposable products are now a mainstay of American enterprise.

Gillette's success grew out of common sense, courage, and a willingness to look at his markets in new ways.

TRY THE UNUSUAL

Alternative media can keep your organizations' names constantly before potential customers. Don't rule out anything as a creative location for advertising: in-store videos, refrigerator magnets, bike racks, trash bins, telephones, airport scheduling screens, ATM receipts, vending machines, taxis, trucks, or floppy disks.

For one day, try looking at everything you see as a place to promote your product or service. If you see it, other people will see it as well.

- Bill McDonald of Highland Park, Illinois, produces weather-safe, velcro-sealed Take-A-Kard cases for business cards that attach to the sides of trucks or cars and carry a message inviting passers-by to lift the flap and take a card from the pouch. McDonald says his cases protect your cards in rain and snow, and at speeds up to 70 miles per hour.

- Fuji found an unlikely place to advertise: inside the minibar refrigerators in guest rooms at San Francisco's Ritz-Carlton Hotel. The company places disposable cameras next to the champagne and guests are charged as they would be for liquor if the cameras are used.

- A sportswear shop offered customers this New Year's Resolution promotion: weigh in at the store, go on a diet, come back on a set date, and for every pound you lose, you earn a 1% discount on clothing and sporting goods.

- Put your photograph on your business cards, flyers, and advertisements to convey the impression that you offer personalized services. Many doctors, chiropractors, and therapists do this, especially if they are not already well known. One chiropractor advertised in flyers and a newspaper ad: "Meet the new doctor in your area . . . I'm Martha D. Bowers, Doctor of Chiropractic. Did you know that to become certified as a chiropractor requires . . ." This informative ad carried a large photo and included a coupon for a free spinal examination, her office hours, and — very prominently — her phone number.

YOUR CUSTOMERS' FAVORITE INNOVATION: MORE FOR THEIR MONEY

It's hard to refuse getting something extra for a small fee, or a second product that makes the first one work better. <u>If you give people more for their money, you can win business from competitors</u> even when you charge more.

- "Bugs" Berger Bug Killers, Inc. of Miami charged much more than competitors for restaurant extermination services. Rather than cut prices, "Bugs" offered an extra service for a small additional fee: cleaning refrigerator coils and resetting insulating seals. Those energy-saving moves saved the restaurants enough money to pay for the higher cost of "Bugs'" pest control.

- Sally McNeal found many new customers for her small word processing business when she began offering extra copies of the documents she prepared at a small additional cost that more than covered her expenses, but was significantly less than her customers would have paid at copy centers.

  In one moment of "applied creativity," as she called it — deliberately sitting down to think of creative ideas that would enhance her business and make it more profitable — she increased her volume by about 10%.

CREATIVE PARTNERSHIPS

<u>When your product and your partner's product share a synergistic relationship</u> — computer hardware and software dealerships, stables and riding gear stores, CPAs and investment consultants — <u>you can offer a "whole greater than the sum of its parts" package.</u>

Some partnerships lend themselves naturally to Walk Your Talk cross-promotion; other brilliant partnerships are **created**:

> Bantam Books had a new romance novel, *The Delaneys of Killaroo*. Clairol had a new hair product, Pazazz Sheer Color Wash. When the book was published, a coupon for 50¢ off on Pazazz (plus a useful booklet on hair-coloring tips) was bundled with it. Packages of Pazazz included a forty-eight-page excerpt from the novel. The heroines, of course, all had hair colors that matched Pazazz's new line.

- A local video store made advertising pay for itself by producing a "coupon book" for local restaurants, events, and retailers (which even included competitors' coupons), stamping its logo on the cover, and attaching a handle so that the book could hang on the front doorknob for easy access — and constant exposure.

CREATE YOUR OWN MEDIA

Create your own advertising media by looking for new places to cross-promote:

- ComputerLand rented the left shoulder of Martina Navratilova's tennis outfit to display their logo. Porsche rented her right shoulder for a while.

- A Duluth television station provides printed "Noon Bulletins" of the day's news and places them next to menus at a local diner. The latest events are printed between two promotional messages at the top and bottom of the page urging people to watch the news when they get home from work.

- Unknown Jerome's cookie customers often keep the bags long after they have eaten the cookies because each one is stamped with a poem by "Jerome."

- As most movie-goers know, products can be featured in films for a fee. That's how Reece's Pieces finally cut into M&M's huge sales lead. They were the candy with which young Elliot lured "E.T." out of the garage. It's no coincidence that movie characters drink particular brands of liquor, drive certain cars, and fly particular airlines.

- Produce your own educational video and make it available at a video rental outlet. Now that more than 50% of all U.S. homes have VCRs, advertisers have discovered the value of video-tapes as advertising media. Colgate-Palmolive sponsors a gourmet cooking tape that mentions its dishwashing detergent. General Foods pays to include Sanka decaffeinated coffee in a health-and-exercise tape. The tapes are either given away as promotional items, or sold at very low prices.

- Create educational or entertaining computer software that customers can use to compare your product or service with others. In 1987, Buick ran ads in computer magazines offering a free diskette in returning a coupon to them. The diskette included a spreadsheet with Buick's prices and options, a graphic image of the dashboard and interior, and a schedule for Buick's payment plans.

- College students earn money by hanging "bikeboards" on their bikes to promote a variety of products. The ads are brokered by a company in Burlingame, California, and the idea is spreading across the state.

GET CUSTOMERS PERSONALLY INVOLVED

Reach out to your customers and get them physically, mentally, and emotionally involved with your product. <u>Find new ways for them to relate to your service</u>. Put yourself in their place and imagine what would make your product or service irresistible.

Give people something personal to keep at your place of business. Bars, restaurants, and even soda fountains give regular customers their own mugs and glasses, which are kept on the premises.

Offer clinics and educational events. You don't even need to take staff time to present these events. Do-it-yourself home improvement clinics can be run at hardware stores by representatives of manufacturers, wholesalers, and distributors whose merchandise is featured in the store. You may be able to work out a similar arrangement.

Help your staff establish ongoing relationships with customers. Encourage the people who work for you to be friendly as well as courteous, and to reach out to customers as individuals. Keep people coming back with a smile, a question about children or family, a reference to what happened last time they were in the store. It costs nothing, makes both your staff and customers feel good, and it's great for business. Those customers will give you more than loyalty; they'll become a word-of-mouth sales force.

SUMMARY

Let your instincts and creativity guide you to unusual and innovative ways to cross-promote your products and services. Target your audience and reach them where they go, regardless of whether or not anyone has gone there before.

REFERENCES
AND SUGGESTED
READINGS

David, Bruce. *Profitable Advertising: A Handbook For Small Business.*

Davidson, Jeffrey. *Marketing on a Shoestring.* John Wiley & Sons. New York. 1988.

Dennison, Dell and Linda Tobey. *The Advertising Handbook.* Self Counsel Press. North Vancouver, British Columbia. 1991.

Hodgson, Richard S. *Successful Catalog Marketing.* Dartnell. Chicago. 1991.

Hotch, Ripley. *How To Start a Business and Succeed.* Stackpole Books. 1991.

Levinson, Jay Conrad. *Guerrilla Marketing: Secrets for Making Big Profits from Your Small Business.* Houghton Mifflin. 1984.

Levinson, Jay Conrad. *Guerrilla Marketing Attack: New Strategies, Tactics & Weapons for Winning Big Profits from Your Small Business.* Houghton Mifflin. 1989.

Meyerowitz, Steven A. *Making a Mark Through Charity or Politics.* Visible Ink Press. 1993.

Ogilvy, David. *Ogilvy on Advertising.* Random House/Vintage Books. 1985.

Phillips, Michael and Salli Rasberry. *Marketing Without Advertising.* Nolo Press. 1986.

Ramacitti, David F. *Do-It-Yourself Publicity.* Amacom/American Management Association. New York. 1991.

Rapp, Stan and Tom Collins. *Maxi-Marketing: The New Direction in Advertising, Promotion, and Marketing Strategy.* Plume. 1988.

Roddick, Anita. *Body and Soul*. Crown. 1991.

Slutsky, Jeff. *Street Fighting: Low Cost Advertising/ Promotions for Your Business*. Available from the author: Retail Marketing Institute, 34 West Whittier Street, Columbus, OH 43206

Slutsky, Jeff with Marc Slutsky. *Street Smart Marketing*. John Wiley & Sons. New York. 1989.

Trout, Jack and Al Riese. *Positioning: The Battle for the Mind*. McGraw Hill. 1986.

Weinrauch, J. Donald. *The Frugal Marketer: Smart Tips for Stretching Your Budget Dollar*. Amacom. 1989.

ORDERING INFORMATION

For individuals:
Our books are available at bookstores, or you are welcome to order from us. Please fill in the order form and return with your check or money order to the address below. You may charge to your VISA or MasterCard by phoning toll-free 1-800-841-2665. Or mail this order form and include:

account number: _____
expiration date: _____
signature: _____

You may also FAX your credit card order to 1-510-559-1629.
Please send me _____ copies of **Walk Your Talk**. I have enclosed $14.95 + $3.50 shipping and handling for *each* copy ordered. California residents please add appropriate sales tax.

Ship to: _____
Name

_____
Address

_____
City/State/Zip Code

Celestial Arts Publishing
P.O. Box 7123
Berkeley, CA 94707   USA